EURIPIDES

WORLD DRAMATISTS

In the same series:

WORLD DRAMATISTS

URIPIDES

SIEGFRIED MELCHINGER

Translated by Samuel R. Rosenbaum

WITH HALFTONE ILLUSTRATIONS

882
Eu 73 Z me

FREDERICK UNGAR PUBLISHING CO.
NEW YORK

*Translated from the original German
and published by arrangement with Friedrich Verlag
Velber, Hannover*

8-75 Puf. 18.50 (7.60)

CONTENTS

CHRONOLOGY

B.C.

and the Areopagus, the last court of appeals, is deprived of its power. Cimon is exiled.

461   Ephialtes is assassinated, and Pericles becomes the leading statesman in Athens.

462–32   The philosopher Anaxagoras teaches in Athens; among his pupils are Pericles and Euripides.

458   Aeschylus's *Oresteia* is performed in Athens. Aeschylus emigrates to Sicily.

456   Aeschylus dies in Sicily.

455   Euripides's *The Peliades*, his first play to be performed at the dionysian dramatic festival, wins third prize.

443   Sophocles becomes treasurer of the Attic Naval League.

442   Sophocles's *Antigone* is performed at the dionysian theater.

441   Euripides emerges for the first time as victor at the dionysian dramatic festival with a play that is not known to us.

438   Euripides's *Alcestis* is performed for the first time in Athens. The Parthenon is dedicated to Pallas Athena.

437   Construction of the Propylaea, on the Acropolis, begins.

431   Euripides's *Medea* is performed in Athens. The Peloponnesian War breaks out between Athens and Sparta.

430 (?)   Euripides's *Children of Heracles* is performed in Athens.

430–29   The plague rages in Athens.

429   Sophocles's *Oedipus the King* is performed at the dionysian theater. Pericles dies of the plague. Nicias becomes the leader of the party

B.C.

of the aristocrats, and Cleon the leader of the democrats.

ca. 428 Euripides's *Hippolytus* is performed in Athens.

427 Aristophanes achieves his first victory at the dionysian dramatic festival. The Spartan troops invade Attica. A punitive expedition against Mytilene is carried out. Plato is born.

425 (?) Euripides's *Hecuba* is performed. Aristophanes's *Acharnians* is performed at the lenaean festival.

421 A peace treaty is signed between Sparta and Athens, known as the Peace of Nicias, who represented Athens. Aristophanes's *The Peace* is performed while the negotiations go on. The stone structure for the theater and the Erechtheum, on the Acropolis, are started.

ca. 421 Euripides's *Heracles* is performed in Athens. His *Cyclops* is performed. *The Suppliant Women* is written.

420 Alcibiades becomes an influential force in Athenian politics.

418 Renewed fighting breaks out between Athens and Sparta.

416 The Athenians attack Melos and massacre the population.

415 Euripides's *The Trojan Women* is performed in Athens.

415–13 The Athenians organize an expedition against Sicily, which ends in disaster for the Athenians. Alcibiades is ostracized by the Athenians and goes over to the enemy side.

ca. 414 Euripides's *Iphigenia in Tauris* is performed.

413 Euripides's *Ion* is performed in Athens. Spar-

B.C.

tans lay siege to Decelea and the war engulfs Attica. Archelaus comes to the throne of Macedonia. A probouleutic council is established in Athens.

ca. 413   Euripides's *Electra* is performed.

ca. 413   Sophocles's *Electra* is performed at the dionysian theater.

412   Euripides's *Helen* is performed in Athens. Many of Athens's allies revolt against her. Sparta forms an alliance with Persia.

411   Aristophanes's *The Thesmophoriazusae* is performed in Athens. Revolution breaks out in Athens and democracy is abolished. Alcibiades is recalled to Athens.

410   Euripides's *The Phoenician Maidens* is performed in Athens. Democracy is restored in Athens. Alcibiades becomes chief admiral of the navy.

409   Sophocles's *Philoctetes* is performed at the dionysian theater.

408   Euripides's *Orestes* is performed.

407   Euripides emigrates to Pella in Macedonia. Alcibiades is deposed.

406   Euripides dies in Pella.

ca. 406   Sophocles dies in Athens.

405   Euripides's *Iphigenia in Aulis* and *The Bacchae* are performed posthumously in Athens. Aristophanes's *The Frogs*, which features Aeschylus, Sophocles, and Euripides in the underworld, is performed in Athens. Athens is surrounded by Spartan and Theban troops.

404   Athens capitulates, which brings an end to the

B.C.

Peloponnesian War. The enemy troops occupy the Acropolis.

401   Sophocles's *Oedipus at Colonus* is produced posthumously at the dionysian theater.

399   Socrates is prosecuted and condemned to death.

THE LIFE AND TIMES
OF EURIPIDES

The Hellenes were not overconcerned about fixing the dates and years of events in their history. They were not averse to making little adjustments in their recitals when required to bring any one event in their history into a meaningful connection with others. For instance, they arranged the chronology of the lives of their three great tragic dramatists —Aeschylus, Sophocles, and Euripides—by basing it on the year of the Battle of Salamis, by far the most memorable event in their annals. It was in that year that Athens gave world history a new direction by defeating the Persians, then one of the great powers of the world. That was in 480 B.C.

They found it satisfying to think that Aeschylus, the oldest of the three, took part in that battle as an officer; that Sophocles, the middle one in years, was on the island as a lad of sixteen and witnessed the evacuation of a large part of the population of Athens to Salamis, when the city went up in flames, although the Persian fleet was completely annihilated; and that Euripides, the youngest of the three, was born on Salamis the very year of the battle.

This chronological coincidence is indeed too pat to be entirely acceptable. Our historians are more apt to rely on 484, a date derived from other sources, as the year of Euripides's birth. Even that year is tied to other events easily enough. For it was in that year that Aeschylus won his first prize in the dionysian dramatic festival, the annual competition in which Athenians bestowed prizes for tragedies on their dramatists.

But is the exact year actually important? Basically, the Hellenic chronology tells us something more worth knowing, which is the general relationship between the three generations involved.

A young man begins, at the age of about sixteen, to take part consciously, if he so wishes, in the public life of the community of which he is a member. This was so in ancient Athens as it is today; yet it was different from other places and other times. Different, because Athens was a relatively small city, in spite of being one of the largest in the world of its time.

Athens had a population of 300,000, of whom about 40,000 had the right to vote and to hold public office. Of the total population, full citizens and their dependents added up to 150,000. In addition, there were 50,000 who did not possess full citizenship because they were aliens or did not hold satisfactory evidence of an Athenian pedigree. There were also, and it is not possible to suppress this shameful statistic, some 100,000 slaves. This averaged out to two slaves to each family, who served as domestics or worked in factories and mines.

We mention the slaves at once because Euripides was one of the first writers who did not take this convenience for granted. It was an established item in the economy, which the Athenians inherited without question from their predecessors. We must realize that there is a difference between personal slavery and the mass enslavement of an entire population. Our century, the century of the annihilation concentration camp and the impersonal prisoner-of-war camp, has little cause for pride. There was mass enslavement in antiquity as well. It was always a threat to the conquered. But personal slavery was also a threat to individuals among the conquered, through more or less public-sale transactions. It was a fact of life then to regard human beings as merchandise and as tools to be bought and sold.

It was during the lifetime of Euripides that, for the first time, people were heard to assert that all men were equal by nature, and that the institution of slavery was just as scandalous as the existence of poverty and wealth. Euripides sided with that opinion. And for that, he was abused by conservatives as a subversive troublemaker.

The victory in the dionysian festival was awarded to him far fewer times than it was to Aeschylus and Sophocles. He won only three times, as against eighteen for Sophocles. His plays were regarded as provocations, and they shocked his contemporaries, but we must not overlook the fact that, at any rate, they were presented, which was in itself a distinction. Even those in the audience who were prone to take offense wanted to see them.

The flag under which Euripides entered public life as a young man was that of opposition. He called out to his contemporaries and his elders: I am determined not to compromise with anything just because it has been that way in the past, whatever it may be. At the time of his youth it was still possible for one to take such a stand.

In that polis, which exercised widely extensive powers though it was relatively small in size, policies were made in the marketplace and on the streets. Everybody of consequence knew everybody else Anyone who had something to say always found listeners. Anyone who desired influence tried to work his way into the legislative body. As in a democracy today, achieving that required one to join one of the parties influential in it. But even that was different.

Democracy in the fourth century B.C. was still comparatively undeveloped in the polis in which it was created. Solon, its great founder, had been dead not quite a hundred years. The constitution he established had been set aside by tyrants after his death, so that the restoration of democracy had occurred less than fifty years before the time that Euripides began to participate in Athenian life. Yet the basic principle of democracy, the freedom and equality of the individual before the law, was preserved and respected, victorious over any rights conferred by grace of the gods, to an extent nobody earlier would have believed possible.

Aeschylus, in the first of his tragedies we still possess, lets the mother of Xerxes, the king of Persia who was defeated at Salamis, ask, about the Athenians: "Who governs them?" She is told: "They do not admit they are vassals or slaves to any man."

Such pride in his polis was manifested also by Sophocles, pride that the power of the laws to preserve freedom and justice was greater than the power of any single individual or than any powers on earth in general. This faith in democracy shines through the plays of both Aeschylus and Sophocles.

This conviction forms the background also of all the plays of Euripides. He never ceased to measure the political realities against the ideals of his polis, even after he began to ask himself whether those realities could ever be anything but tragic, considering the basic characteristics of human nature and the basic requirements of existence in a community. But this skepticism and pessimism did not hinder him, even as an old man, from writing tragedies for his contemporaries in which he demonstrated that he was still not prepared to reconcile himself with practical realities. (We should keep in mind that none of the three great Athenian dramatists ever had a play performed a second time in the Athenian theater because of the ruling that only new works could be offered. No exception to this rule occurred until after the death of Aeschylus.)

The young Euripides who first entered public life had enjoyed the well-rounded upbringing that was customary for every young man from a good Athenian home. There was no aspect of community activity with which he had not been made familiar. This too was one of the advantages of the young democracy as it then existed, which has now vanished never to return. He grew up on his family's estate on Salamis. He frequented the town hall that was the meeting place of the land-owning families in the exclusive suburb of Phyla there. He performed the services in religion, sports, the arts, and the army expected from one in his station in life. He took part in the dances and carried a torch in the festivals of Apollo, and he won prizes in competition as an athlete. He is also said to have had some success as a painter, which is interesting, as we know practically nothing about Hellenic painting beyond what went into the decoration of pottery. It is just at that period, however, that the famous mural painter Polygnotus flourished, and the arts must by then have attained the high level we can observe in the extant sculptures.

The allusion to athletic prizes allows us to conjecture that Euripides must have attended the games at Olympia. Phidias maintained a studio there that we can still see today in which he worked on the famous pediments on the temple of Zeus. The sculptures on these pediments, with the incredibly lovely figure of Apollo among them, must be studied to appreciate how the dramatists visualized the characters in their tragedies.

When the time came for Euripides to decide which career he would follow, he had gathered experiences to make the most momentous resolution in his life: he decided to withdraw entirely from public life. He chose for himself the platform of the dramatist, on which not he himself but his work would be exposed to the public.

From that point on we know practically nothing about his personal life. He accepted no more public office and rendered no more military service, differing in this respect from Aeschylus and Sophocles. His withdrawal from public affairs was attributed by his critics to contempt for people and the world. As a result of the high degree of his erudition he incurred the reputation of being a bookworm. Popular gossip about his private life flourished, as it always does about an individual who turns his back on the world. He must have had some good reason for abstaining from politics. I can only guess that it was possibly due to events that occurred before he made his decision.

In 462, when Euripides was twenty-two (if he was born in 484), the party of the democrats seized power in Athens under the leadership of Ephialtes and Pericles. It was a bloody coup d'état. The elimination of the aristocracy made powerless the Areopagus, the last court of appeals. One was appointed to it not by lot or by election but by virtue of the esteem in which one was held. As a matter of fact it had remained a prerogative of the aristocrats. Solon had hoped to keep the Areopagus free of democratic processes in order to have some stable instrument that could hold fast against the constant changes of opinions and the power struggles of political factions. Now it lost its supervisory function and its jurisdiction was limited to matters of capital punishment.

We know from Aeschylus's last trilogy, his *Oresteia*, performed in 458, four years after Ephialtes and Pericles seized power, how seriously and apprehensively he criticized this violent overturn, in the light of the previously accepted ideas of the polis. No limits were set any longer to the authority of the party in power. Aeschylus felt the time had come for him to go into exile. In that year he emigrated to Sicily and died there in 456.

Nevertheless, the great period of Athens, as it is described by the historians, began at that time, perhaps the greatest. Yet, at least after the assassination of Ephialtes in 461, it could better be described as the great period of one man, Pericles. Sophocles was his friend, but Sophocles was not a fellow traveler with the party in power. He arrogated to himself the right to criticize and warn, a right that was conceded to the writer of tragedy until the last years of freedom in Athens. He warned his friend to avoid the hubris that power brings. It is evidence of the greatness of Pericles that he permitted the warning and respected the accepted practices of democracy as he did the established traditions of religion. He was not like Creon in *Antigone*, whom Sophocles portrayed as a dictator. Instead, though Pericles was the leader of Athens, he submitted each year to the elective process. Even though he was no longer a believer in the gods (Thucydides, historian of the period, never even quoted any mention of the gods in his reports of the speeches of Pericles), Pericles initiated the building of the Parthenon, a majestic tribute to the gods. In its innermost chamber a larger-than-life statue of Athena in ivory and gold by Phidias was erected. No religious services were ever held in the temple, nor was the statue the object of religious veneration. It stood as a tribute to the illusion of religion that ruled the Hellenic world.

If nowhere else, we see in this the popular belief that must have animated the opposition of Euripides. One of his basic themes was the unmasking of the illusions of religion by which men live, which he tried to accomplish by demonstrating to his contemporaries the influence on them of what he believed was an illusion.

We have nothing but his work itself from which to draw this conclusion. We lack any hard facts about his life until its end was near. Even the dates of production of his plays are in question, save for four of them, one of which was posthumous. Nevertheless, what we have of his works is far more extensive than what has survived from the two older tragedians. We have only seven plays by Aeschylus and seven by Sophocles, whereas we have eighteen by Euripides. (Another one, *Rhesus*, usually ascribed to him, is certainly not authentic.) We know the titles of fifty-six that he had performed, and we have considerable fragments of many of those. We can calculate that the polis "granted him a chorus," to use the official phrase, on at least twenty-two occasions. As this meant a tetralogy on each such occasion (three tragedies and a satyr play), a minimum of eighty-eight of Euripides's dramas must have been performed.

Should this relative richness of material not permit us to draw some indirect conclusions about his life and work? Indeed, such research has been attempted, but no sound results have come from it. A whole philosophy has been constructed by stringing together quotations from his plays, for even in antiquity he was regarded as the "skenikos philosophos," the dramatist-philosopher.

But the dramatists of antiquity are objective, as all great dramatists are. They do not speak through their characters. Every passage in which an opinion, a thought, or a maxim is expressed, can be understood only in relation to the situation in which it appears. The only inquiry that is relevant is to examine who it is that says what, and when. None of the plays contains a "lesson" to be drawn from it.

In his day Euripides was famous for the quotable phrases that abound in his plays. Certainly many of them are reflections of his wide reading, which can be traced to the writings of others, and contemporary colloquialisms. But even the most significant statements of philosophy in his plays are opinions of the characters who speak them, not the philosophy of the play as a whole. Euripides usually had his characters give voice to opinions then shared by many of his contemporaries.

Only in one of his plays, and that to only a limited extent, are there factual aspects of history, in the sense that Brecht used the phrase. All the others put mythical events on the stage, using them as though they were contemporaneous.

And yet there is an element of biography in every one of the plays we possess. We can hardly evade the question of why he selected the particular issue, time, and characters he chose to dramatize. Consideration of how he hoped a play would affect his audience reveals more to us about his opinions and intentions than stitching together a thousand quotations with inadequate information about his life.

We can, however, with some degree of certainty, assign periods of his life to separate the earlier plays from his later productions. This will hardly give us an exact time table or fix dates of events with any accuracy. But one insight changed his thinking and writing.

We owe it to a fortunate, certainly not accidental, circumstance that we know, in at least one respect, more about the life of Euripides than we do about the lives of Aeschylus and Sophocles, though it is little enough.

We see him in person walking about the streets and sitting at his desk at home. Perhaps he does not appear there quite as he really was, but at any rate, we can see him as the greater number of his contemporaries saw him or wanted to. We see him possibly as if in a distorted mirror, but even the most real existence in the present is often seen as if distorted.

In 423, when Euripides was in his sixties or going on sixty, an actor appeared in a mask representing him on the stage where his plays were being presented. A comedy by Aristophanes, a young playwright then not quite twenty years old, who had made quite a stir, was being performed. The play was his *Acharnians*, about peasants in the north of Attica who at that time were being forced by one of the frequent invasions of the Spartans to live as refugees within the walls of Athens. The hero, a charcoal burner with the expressive name of Dicaeopolis (which means in Hellenic approximately a man of the city of laws) strikes a separate peace for himself with the Spartans and is therefore called to account by his more patriotic fellow countrymen. Before his trial he asks one favor. He wishes to be allowed to put on the ragged costume of a beggar, so that he can in the elevated style of tragedy better excite sympathy.

This is the cue for the entry of Euripides, who was famous for having a hero appear in beggar's costume, whether he was a deposed king in flight from his pursuers, or a shipwrecked prince, or someone in disguise who wished to gain access to his enemies without being recognized. Dicaeopolis names five such heroes, whom we have no knowledge of.

The satire was effectively staged. The stage setting is the house of Euripides. Dicaeopolis, who wishes to borrow a beggar costume from Euripides, knocks on the door. A slave answers the door sullenly. Asked if the master of the house is at home, the slave replies: "He is and he isn't." "What do you mean by that?" asks Dicaeopolis. The slave explains: "In spirit, he is away, because he is up in the clouds when he is writing poetry. But he himself is at home." Naturally, he must not be disturbed. Dicaeopolis calls out aloud: "Euripides, my good kind Euripides!" A voice answers from within: "I have no time for you!" But Euripides relents. He lets himself be rolled out. Then we see the theater machine put into use, one that Aeschylus had previously used—a wooden platform on wheels that could be rolled out on the stage. It was mostly brought out for the bloody and gruesome events.

This must have caused a storm of laughter and applause when it was rolled out in this comedy. The famous dramatist is seen at his desk in his study, whose walls are so hung over with beggar costumes that it looks like a second-hand store. Euripides himself, with stylus in hand, is himself dressed in a beggar costume, so that he can properly write himself into a new role.

Dicaeopolis, on his knees, begs for one of the costumes. Euripides impatiently offers him one after another. First he suggests that of Oineus, a poor old man. "No, that won't do. It must be something far more wretched than that." "Then, take the costume of Phoenix, the blind man." "No, something much worse." "Then try this Bellerophon, all covered with mud." "No, it must be like all of them together. I must be a lame beggar, a vagabond and a boaster." "Ah, now I know what you want: Telephos!" "Yes, that's it, something all in tatters."

Dicaeopolis scrounges together all the properties he

needs by quoting extracts from Euripides's plays; a beggar's staff, a half-broken jug, a pot with a sponge in it, a sooty little basket. "But my good fellow," Euripides protests, "you are depriving me of all my tragedies."

But the last bit is the worst. "Euripidearie, my heart's blood, my little sugar sweetness! You don't often get a chance to do such a good noble deed. I only want one more little thing. Oh, give me some chervil out of what your mother left you!" This slur on his mother (accusing her of having been a lowly market gardener) hits Euripides below the belt, and he orders Dicaeopolis evicted from the house.

This cheap but effective joke was based on the gossip that vegetables grown on the estate of Euripides's parents on Salamis were offered for sale in the markets of Athens. Later this was magnified into a legend that his mother had been a market woman. The scene can be relished because it shows how even a great dramatist could be made the butt of ridicule in Athens by having his private life lampooned.

It shows also that he was a famous man in spite of his lack of success in getting the first prize in the annual dionysian dramatic festival. Aristophanes had previously taken aim at him in an earlier comedy, and later did so again in others.

In one of them the subject is again a costume, this time a woman's frock. The women of Athens determine to start a lawsuit against Euripides because he insults their sex. He persuades one of his relatives to worm his way disguised as a woman into the court of justice to plead his case for him. This changing of clothes is presented in a very circuitous and highly indecent manner. Then the lawsuit opens. Every possible indecency is charged to the defendant—adultery, pederasty, deceitfulness, drunkenness, hysteria. But a peddler of holy pictures takes the cake, claiming that she has lost half her business since he, the rascal, has been persuading people with his verses that there are no more gods.

We note that even in his lifetime Euripides was a subject of gossip and controversy among the masses. Later, so-called historians, in all seriousness, charged that his second wife deceived him with a handsome young slave who was his secretary. In this manner, they pushed his story, so to speak, into the same bed as that of Phaedra and Hippolytus, with which he won a first prize when he used it as the plot for one of his tragedies. It was, in fact, true that the play was one of the shocks he administered to his contemporaries, when he brought a woman like Phaedra on the stage, who, driven by unrequited love, shamelessly tries to throw herself into the arms of a much younger man, her own stepson. An authority no less than Pericles had laid down the rule that the requirement of a good woman is that, among men, she be spoken about as little as possible, whether for good or ill.

The polis was a man's world. Women were supposed to have no business in its public life. They were regarded with so little esteem that we can hardly understand it today. No one found it remarkable if a man left his wife and children to live with another woman or with a friend. But woe to any woman who dared to do the same thing! In his *Medea* Euripides was the first among the tragic playwrights to defend the right of the wife to expect humane treatment. It was precisely this position that was taken amiss by his society, including the women who respected the dictum of Pericles. The label of woman-hater was hung on him by the conformists, to turn women against him. How excellently this strategy succeeded is taught by Aristophanes's comedy *The Thesmophoriazusae* (411).

The charge that he persuaded people that there were no gods any longer might have had dangerous consequences, as could be seen by the prosecution and execution of Socrates in 399, seven years after Euripides's death. Such suits, charging impiety or godlessness, became more frequent as Athens approached its downfall. They were often brought cynically as weapons in the conflict for political power.

It throws a lurid light on the decline of democracy to find that such denunciations could be effective in doing in political opponents or others one wanted to injure. The slanderers went so far as to even bring charges against Aeschylus, who was put to considerable pains to defend such a suit. Euripides is said to have been similarly accused, but in any case there was no guilty verdict. In the next chapter I shall discuss what he thought about the gods, but it will help us to understand the times in which he lived if we keep in mind an awareness of the sort of expression that was considered dangerous and at which Aristophanes openly aimed his barbs.

The second half of the fifth century is repeatedly described as the period of the Hellenic enlightenment. Two notable scholars attached to Euripides the label that still clings to him today, "the dramatist of the enlightenment," or "the rationalist." Hellenic enlightenment had started much before the time of Euripides. As I pointed out previously it is always a mistake to believe that a particular speech reflects a dramatist's belief. Scripts of actors' separate parts got out into the hands of readers, who assumed that they contained passages expressing the beliefs of Euripides.

If, by the term "enlightenment," we mean the mastery of self of every thinking man in the face of all that is unknowable and not manifest, that striving for truth that occupied the minds of thinking Hellenes ever since the sixth century and led to the highest intellectual accomplishments of philosophical investigation, then Euripides was a "man of the enlightenment." But, if so, Aeschylus and Sophocles were, as well.

The homeric view of the world had collapsed. The conception of gods had been transformed. The old legends were no longer literally believed. This is not to imply that people no longer believed in any god at all, or in the concept of divinity. But they recognized that behind the old names and the anthropomorphic figures were powers affecting the existence of mankind, to which no tangible causes or obvious purposes could be rationally ascribed. It was the basic belief of tragedy that our existence on earth is surrounded by an unknowable, which visits its blows upon the guilty and the innocent alike. This is the central perception of the tragedians.

None of the three great dramatists drew the conclusion that the only recourse left for mankind was to accept supinely, without resisting, the forces that are arrayed against it, or to hope for redemption in some future life. Aeschylus and Sophocles showed that they favored such resistance by their active participation in political life and public affairs.

We know that Euripides's response was different,

but this does not signify that his study, in which Aristophanes has him rolled out on the stage, was in an ivory tower. On the contrary, he withdrew into it in order to attack the conduct of public affairs all the better. Every one of his plays is written for the public. Even in his latest dramas, all the conflicts are political to some degree. His theater is a theater of society, political theater. In this respect Euripides was neither a hermit nor an aesthete; he was a writer who wanted to enlighten. But he was not by any means a sophist.

Sophistry was the system of thought that was attracting Hellenic intellectuals with increasing force during the second half of the fifth century. Only later did "sophistry" degenerate into what we call sophistry today, that is, hypercritical casuistry and crafty dissimulation.

At first only those thinkers were called sophists who made it a career to cultivate their ability to think, the professional philosophizers. They taught everything that could be done with the mind. They established the theorems of mathematics and science, and also the principles of law, and, above all, the art of speech, or rhetoric.

The last played a dominating role in the polis of that day because it ruled not only the proceedings in the legislature but also the practice of law in the courts. The methods of argumentation, the sequence of arriving at deductions from given facts, were thoroughly studied and constantly refined until at last the arguments themselves were regarded as facts that themselves could be manipulated.

The teachers instructed their pupils in the art of looking at any subject from both sides. They spread the view that in fact every subject had its two sides. They consequently arrived at the point of seeking out not the truth of any statement but only the attractiveness and credibility of any line of reasoning. They came to regard public acceptance of an opinion as more important than the search for intrinsic truth itself.

In no other period has the power of thought held greater sway over men. Anaxagoras spoke of it as "bios theoretikos," a life of theory, a life of thought. Protagoras, the instructor of a whole school of sophists, applied his maxim that "man is the measure of all things" to start the transvaluation of all values. It had the effect of causing everything handed down from before, even the constitution and the laws, to be assessed relatively, not accepted absolutely. This led to the differentiation between "physis" and "nomos," between nature and law or morals. It encouraged youth to assert unequivocally the primacy of the rights of nature. The proposition of the innate right of the stronger to prevail developed at first only into meaning the right of the stronger in intellect, but its application to public life, especially in politics, brought fateful consequences with it.

Alcibiades who, more than any other public figure, governed himself by the political principles Machiavelli was to lay down many centuries later, was a pupil of the sophists. Euripides, in his Eteocles in *The Phoenician Maidens*, presents a ruler who ruthlessly disregards considerations of morality, putting his will to exert power above all moral principles. He is a "superman," whom Nietzsche may have studied. Not unexpectedly, Euripides causes him to come to grief.

None of the ideas that were current in this period fail to find expression in the tragedies. Euripides knew the thoughts of the philosophers and the sophists as though he were himself one of them. Tradition says that he was in personal contact with Socrates, and it is probable that Protagoras delivered lectures in his home.

We have inherited a warm remark made by Socrates—that he would be willing to walk the five miles from Athens to Piraeus to witness a play by Euripides in the theater where his plays were then being performed.

But we shall see that Euripides did not share either the optimistic belief that the world would eventually be set in order through progressive enlightenment, or the sophistical theories about the right of the stronger to prevail. He had his own individual point of view. He was a writer of tragedies.

We can best appreciate Euripides as a political man by focusing on the turning point that is discernible in his oeuvre and at which we hinted before.

After the death of Pericles in 429, the year of the plague in Athens, the influence of the sophists caused a fermentation of the germs of conflict that began to work on the intellectual youth of the polis. Eventually it resulted in an explosion and revolt that the authority of Pericles had prevented.

Democracy is the form of government by the "polloi," the many, that is, by the majority of them. In a democracy, as in any form of government, the intellectuals will always be in the minority. Their claim to control as an elite can only be realized if they can convince the majority that they are worthy of it.

It follows that anyone who strives to attain power must win the favor of the multitude. Two more conclusions are equally convincing.

One is that, after the failure of an enterprise, if approval of the masses for it has been obtained by persuasion, the masses will take revenge on those who have turned out to be seducers instead of leaders. The second is that, after a serious catastrophe, the multitude tries to shrug off its responsibility for the enterprise and to blame it on such a minority, or even on an individual leader.

It was this latter tendency that marked the political development in Athens. A shrewd observer who was witness to this state of affairs could not remain silent when he could predict the consequences toward which it was inevitably heading. To him, war as a continuation of national politics, as, that is, the Peloponnesian War would be, was just as senseless as promoting war for imperialistic goals, the kind of war introduced by Pericles and for which he still had to account.

At a historic moment, after the peace among equals —Athens and Sparta—known as the Peace of Nicias had been signed in 421, providing for the mutual return of war prisoners and war booty, when there seemed again to be an opportunity to renounce war and avoid its worst consequences, Euripides decided to write a major political tragedy. It was *The Suppliant Women*. We do not know what was directly responsible for its composition. It is not unlikely that he received a commission from the polis to write it.

In this play Euripides affirmed his belief in the vitality of Solon's democracy. Theseus, as spokesman for the polis and its people, acts on the principle—a concept as great as it is realistic—that the political man is at liberty to choose the better over the worse course (not just the good over the bad). He praises the accomplishments of man: Man has learned to speak and to communicate. He has learned to till the fields and build cities and sail the seas. "But is it not sacrilege if we refuse to be content with what we can do and strive to rate man's reason above divine power? Is it not sacrilege if we allow the hubris that dwells in man's hearts to assert that he is wiser than the gods?"

This exhortation, not at all mythical, repeats the moral of the warning by Aeschylus in the *Oresteia*— that, in civic policy, we must never lose sight of "that which is to be held in awe."

The warning against hubris given in *The Suppliant Women* turned out to be fruitless. History took its inevitable course. From then on, Euripides lost his belief in the future of the polis. He became deeply skeptical about the future of men.

As Athens declined, Euripides's tragedies grew more and more pessimistic. They pointed to the true motives of the great, of those who make history. They showed the visage behind the mask, the true character behind the appearances and the labels with which men conceal their selfish interests, their personal ambition, their striving for power, as they try to win popular support, to take advantage of the willingness of the masses to be misled, the masses whose feelings constitute, or can be manipulated into forming, public opinion.

This is the foreground and the background of life

in the polis, the life of the community as it actually is, the status of man as the wolf to his fellowman, or the wolf's victim if he is not the wolf.

In 415 (and we know that date with certainty), a few years after *The Suppliant Women*, Euripides brought his *Trojan Women* to the stage of the dionysian theater. After World War I, Wilamowitz-Moellendorf, the great classical scholar, asked the question: "How was it possible that Euripides could have wished to present this drama to his fellow countrymen?" What could have happened in those years to account for his offering *The Trojan Women* after *The Suppliant Women*, a funeral lament after such a hymn of praise? In *The Trojan Women* Troy is in the same plight that Athens is to be in after the Peloponnesian War. When the closing scene of *The Trojan Women* was presented, the Acropolis, at the foot of which the audience sat, was set ablaze. It was a warning, a mene tekel! In the play the women are driven into slavery. But even more awful to contemplate than the sufferings of the victims were the cynicism, the lack of morality, and the cruelty of the victors. After ten years of war, a great patriotic war for the fatherland, your homeric war of heroes, what happened to your men? They became beasts.

In the same year, 415, the Sicilian expedition set sail from Athens. Three months after the presentation of *The Trojan Women* the greatest fleet that Athens had ever assembled set out westward into the Mediterranean, carrying a heavily armed expeditionary force. It was sheer aggression. The pretext of responding to a call for aid from an ally was so threadbare it was absurd. Athens had degenerated to that low a level. No effort even had to be made to disguise this cynical exercise of power politics and the right of the stronger to prevail. What were the war aims? Simply to eliminate Sparta (with which a fifty-year peace had been signed) forever as a rival in the Mediterranean, and to ravage the boundless wealth of Sicily, to get spoils every citizen hoped to share. The historian Alfred Heuss has rendered this verdict on the campaign:

> The plans they made were rife with error. They were fascinating and promised a handsome return. All the problems that had beset Athens for nearly half a century were to be solved at one stroke. This thought was incredibly electrifying. The Athenians were possessed by it as by a fixed idea. Previously, Athens would have been protected from such a project because it would have encountered the automatic resistance of an opposition party, but now it was almost unanimously approved. It stirred the people up into downright delirium. Even if there were some left who kept a cool head, few dared to speak their mind.

Euripides did dare to speak. The man who had put the idée fixe into Athenian minds was a warmongering genius, Alcibiades. A disputed tradition would have us believe that one year before *The Trojan Women* was produced, Euripides extolled a victory of Alcibiades in the Olympic games with one of the customarily commissioned hymns of praise. If that was true, the composition of *The Trojan Women* would seem to indicate that he must have torn up this hymn and thrown it at the feet of Alcibiades, when the latter became a war incendiary.

In one of the speeches delivered by Alcibiades that Thucydides himself heard and reported in his *History*, he said:

> Let us go forth with our attack so we can magnify our power! We want a final victory over the Spartans. The might of any state is wasted away in time of peace. It is my positive conviction that a state accustomed to activity must decline if it devotes itself to repose.

By "repose" he meant "peace."

Thucydides shows what the Athenians were capable of doing in time of peace in an instance he cites together with the agitation to go to war in 416–415. It is the cynical invasion of the island of Melos, which had committed no offense against Athens except that it had refused to sell its freedom. Athens occupied the island. The whole male population was butchered. The women and children were sold into slavery. Thucydides quotes the Melian envoys as asking: "Is it really not perilous for Athens to violate every rule of right? Empires too are mortal."

That was the question Euripides flung into the delirium of the public mind with his *Trojan Women* when there was still time for reflection. It might as well have been flung into the winds.

The catastrophe of the Sicilian expedition was complete. Athens never recovered from this defeat. Sicily was to it what Stalingrad was to Hitler. The massacre was so frightful that the waters of the rivers ran red with blood. Generals were executed. Prisoners were driven by the thousands into the notorious Latonian caves, which became their prisons.

The news caused panic in Athens. The dismay and terror were indescribable. Every inhabitant was afflicted both as a citizen and in his private life. The uncertainty as to the fate of individuals, the fathers, sons, and grandsons, the husbands and brothers, paralyzed the life of the city. Alcibiades was banished even before the end of the campaign. He defected to Sparta.

For a short while after the prudent minority had the upper hand. A probouleutic council was set up of prominent leaders, of whom Sophocles was one. They took over the direction of the government. But the consequences of the defeat began to afflict the polis. The Spartans occupied Decelea, only eleven miles north of the city, from which they could control all of the polis outside of Athens. The rural population fled for safety inside the city, which was soon congested with refugees. The polis funds were rapidly depleted by the doles that had to be distributed to the unemployed. Building construction at the Erechtheum on the Acropolis was continued only to provide work for those in need. The silver mines at Laurium were in the hands of the enemy. Spartan troops were pillaging the country close to the gates of Athens.

It was Alcibiades who had devised the diabolical plan of drawing away the financial reserves of Athens and of breaking her will to resist through the military occupation of Decelea. The fluctuation in public opinion about Alcibiades is more clearly reflected in Euripides's later plays. He was alternately banished (then he served as adviser to the enemy) and again recalled, again banished, and once more recalled.

In 413 a revolution broke out in Athens. Anti-democratic radicals overturned the probouleutic council. The rabble, no longer restrained, took the macabre step, at an assembly on the hill at Colonus, of voting to abolish the democracy. It was a wave of reaction, or, one might say, fascism, that won this victory. General public sentiment swung around against the social reformers. Persecutions were instituted. The philosopher Anaxagoras was able, by precipitate flight, to escape the fate that threatened him, which was later visited upon Socrates. The respected sophist Protagoras was drowned at sea when he took flight. His books were publicly burned. The charge against him was the same as that leveled against Euripides in the comedy by Aristophanes then being played: blasphemy. It is true that democracy was reinstituted later, but history could not be stopped.

Relentlessly Euripides continued on his chosen path, the path of exposing the guilty, as is to be seen in the eulogy he wrote on commission from the polis for those who had been lost in Sicily.

In one single play, the longest of his extant tragedies, *The Phoenician Maidens*, Euripides treated the whole saga of Oedipus and his sons. He seems to be saying: "See now, what greatness amounts to, what heroism is, and fame, and what there is behind all these concepts!"

As Sartre said, "Euripides utilized these hackneyed words in order to demolish them from within." There is some truth in this analysis, even if Sartre's conclusion cannot be fully sustained. For instance, Euripides's attitude toward belief in the gods must be treated differently, but of this more will be said in the next chapter.

At the same time, Euripides attacked the accepted political platitudes. In his *Orestes* he shows the low estate to which democracy had fallen, in his picture of a people's court that took place. (True enough, it is placed in Argos, but it is conducted exactly as if it were taking place in Athens.) Demagogues and opportunists have the last word. Public opinion is manipulated in the corridors of power. The voice of pure reason is scattered to the winds.

Hellenic democracy was in decline. As in *Orestes*, great legal trials were decided in a people's court. The law courts, as Victor Ehrenberg described the situation, "became a playground for orators and sycophants,* a development that seems to have taken place in Argos even earlier than in Athens. This then was the terminal

---

* *In ancient Athens the Hellenic word that is translated as sycophant had a very specific meaning. It referred to a breed of people who practiced slander, blackmail, tale-bearing, informing as a regular profession. The sycophant put on patriotic airs; he haled people into court for all sorts of alleged crimes against the state because of his claimed loyalty to the polis and the established laws. Actually, he extorted money from victims because the political structure of the polis allowed any citizen to defame another by instituting proceedings against him. Every man of position and means lived in perpetual terror of this tribe because the accusation put him in danger of banishment, ostracism, expropriation, and jail as the judges decreed.*

Since no shame was attached to the leveling of slanderous charges, the sycophant flourished with impunity. While it is true that he was liable to a fine of one thousand drachmas if he failed to win one-fifth of the judges' votes, it was easy enough to get more than that number to go along in a state that, having become deified, looked upon even minor deviations as acts of sacrilege. In the rare event that a sycophant was fined, in practice he did

phase of her democracy: the masses became the judges of all causes and democracy itself was utterly discredited."

In *Orestes* Euripides's purpose in presenting a suit by the people of Argos against Orestes was to point up the way the administration of justice in Athens was being abused by those who had political power. Only the unbelievably implicit respect with which the Athenians regarded their theater and their tragic dramatists could allow Euripides to hazard the foolhardiness of this provocation.

But it seems that Euripides had gone too far this time. A year after *Orestes* was produced, he was living in exile. He took the same road Aeschylus was forced to take after his *Oresteia*. And he was to die in Macedonia a year and a half later.

It was a laborious journey for Euripides, then seventy-seven years old, but he was rewarded by the flattering attention showered upon him. He spent his last years in what was a palace of the muses. Pella, near today's Saloniki, was the seat of the tyrant Archelaus, who garnered famous names to add luster to his power and his wealth. The painter Zeuxis, the composer Timotheus, perhaps also the historian Thucydides, certainly Agathon, a younger rival of Euripides in the tragic theater, were guests at that time in his court. Euripides showed his gratitude by

---

not have to pay the fine. We have records of sycophants who allowed fines to accumulate without being subjected to any penalty for failure to pay. It proves the extraordinary vitality of the Athenian polis that it survived despite the evil that sycophancy spread.

making a mythical ancestor of Archelaus the hero of a drama, now lost. His creative power was undiminished.

We have two magnificent plays of the last trilogy he wrote while he lived at Pella, *Iphigenia in Aulis* and *The Bacchae*. Homesickness for Athens does not betray itself in a single line of either of these. *Iphigenia in Aulis* continues the debunking of the renowned heroes of antiquity. Some passages recited by the chorus praise the beauty of the land in which he found asylum.

The Bacchae, rated by many his finest creation, is also without doubt the most enigmatic. Not one of his earlier works known to us can be compared with it. Composed at the same time as Sophocles's *Oedipus at Colonus*, this play constitutes the final keystone of the arch of the tragic drama.

Euripides was dead when *The Bacchae* was produced in Athens. The polis was under siege. The Peloponnesian War was lost, and with it freedom came to an end.

But the theater was still playing. The dionysian festival was just getting underway when the news of Euripides's death reached the city. At the formal opening of the festival, Sophocles, then ninety years old, came forward in the proagon, the traditional opening ceremony. He wore mourning garb. The actors left off the wreaths with which custom ordained they be adorned and wore black cloaks. The polis was united once more to do honor to their great dead.

Tradition has it that Euripides was torn to death by Archelaus's hunting dogs while he was away on an outing. That was one of the tales rich in implications of the kind the Hellenes loved, for the hero of his last tragedy, *The Bacchae*, was also torn apart by beasts (in human form).

For centuries after his death, Euripides's grave was displayed to visitors to Macedonia. The Athenians erected a monument to him. But a most hilarious tribute was paid him in the last year that freedom was allowed to comedy on the stage.

Aristophanes, in his *Frogs* (405), let him appear in the underworld. No less a figure than Dionysus goes there to pay him his last respects. He finds Euripides in the middle of a lawsuit. Euripides is demanding the throne of the leading tragedian of the world, occupied by Aeschylus. Sophocles, who was already dead, had, on entering Hades, kissed the hand of Aeschylus, conceding him the throne. In this way the stage is set for one of the most devastating satires ever written— Aristophanes's account of the contest between Euripides and Aeschylus. Euripides boasts of what he did for language and thought. Aeschylus does not deny his claims; his defense is that Euripides did indeed do all he lays claim to—but that he should not have done any of it.

Euripides was both a great and a highly controversial figure in his lifetime. His reputation began to grow after his death. His star acquired the brightest glow of the three in the galaxy of tragedy.

The report that the prisoners taken in the siege of Syracuse in the Sicilian expedition sang Euripides's choral songs in the caves in which they were imprisoned, and that the Sicilians, captivated by the beauty of the music, granted the prisoners their freedom, can be likened to an epitaph for his tomb in the hearts of the Athenians.

THE THEATER OF ATHENS

At the time Euripides was writing his first tragedies, plays were being produced for fifty years in the declivity on the south slope of the Acropolis of Athens, where the ruins of the dionysian theater can still be seen today. The arena had been moved there from within Athens proper because the urban arenas were not large enough to accommodate the crowds who attended. We can only guess at the seating capacity of the theater, as not all the tiers and seats have been preserved. It seems likely there were seats for at least 14,000, probably even 17,000 spectators. This was not enough to take care of the whole population, not even a fourth or fifth of it, but even in those days there were many more who were more interested in sporting events or other forms of entertainment than in theater.

The theater was so highly esteemed, however, that it had been taken under the protection of the polis. Every spring, when the new wine was maturing in the vats, the festival of Dionysus, the god of wine, of intoxication, of transformation, the god of the theater, was celebrated. It was in his honor that the annual presentation of dramas was named the dionysian dramatic festival. There was a temple of the god close by the theater. Archaeologists have excavated the foundations of both an older and a newer temple. The cult of Dionysus began in an earlier era. The festival conducted in his name in the fifth century as an established institution was the end product of a development of tradition and convention that, at a time even earlier, had burst like a volcanic eruption out of emotional depths previously suppressed, out of subterranean abysses. The eruption would send his worshippers forth in one furious debauch. In *The Bacchae*, Euripides's last play, we see how such an orgy develops into the stuff of tragedy.

Dionysus, who also appears there as a character, calls such orgies consecrations to himself. As the communicants were aroused into a state of manic excitement, the throng of celebrants were called maenads. Another name of the god was Bacchus. He was also referred to as Bromius, the noisemaker or roisterer. The Romans reduced Bacchus to the status of being only the god of wine.

The word "tragedy" means literally "goat song." As late as in classic times, theater tradition required every presentation to end with a satyr play. The satyrs wore goatskins, as do the bacchantes in Euripides. Some say that originally Dionysus was an embodiment of the spring, so that his recurring return was celebrated as a symbol of nature's annual renewal. This may have been so in early antiquity, but as early as the sixth century B.C. he was appearing in a new guise as a god in his victory processions. He seemed to be emerging from the distant past, a strange and terrifying figure, as if he were a barbarian, in the costume provided for him by Euripides.

He released drives in the spirit of men that were usually repressed by the customary restraints of communal life. He liberated inhibitions usually dammed up. It is likely that such religious eruption bore a direct relationship to the desire of the lower classes to break bonds set up against them by the caste system of the aristocrats.

At about the same time, the self-assertion of the human mind through philosophy and science was beginning to flourish in Hellas. The political genius of the Hellenes manifested itself in the way they brought both movements under control and domesticated them. What was unchained was put in new fetters: cultic forms and the restraints of art.

It is significant that the priests of the temple at Delphi, in which Apollo, one of the greatest of the "old" gods was worshipped, received the assignment to institutionalize the new cult of Dionysus. In consequence, the pediment of the largest temple at Delphi was adorned, as Nietzsche interpreted it, by the figures of Apollo and of Dionysus. Phidias, who created the unbelievably beautiful Apollo of Delphi, also created a Dionysus, which lay recumbent in a pediment of the Parthenon at Athens, and can be seen today, alas, badly preserved, in the British Museum in London.

Euripides, who was supposed to be the rationalist and man of enlightenment, still knew enough about the origins of tragedy to dedicate to Dionysus *The Bacchae*. The dionysian impulse, though long restrained by religious rites and observances, permeated the action through to the very end of the play in every performance. It burst forth in the characters on the stage when they lost control of themselves or were overcome by the tumult of their innermost passions.

There is no tragedy without such inner mania, such orgy or fury, such unchaining of passions. Aristotle later defined this as the true function of the theater, because it causes a catharsis, a purification, that he likened to medical purgation. In fact, theater and the art of healing were often closely bound together in those days, as we can still verify. This can be seen in Epidaurus, where the most beautiful and the best-preserved Greek theater, dating from the third century B.C., stands very close to the place where Asclepius, the god of the medical art, was worshipped and healing took place. On the southern slope of the Acropolis, similar establishments of health and worship were likewise directly connected with the theater. As the first priest of Asclepius, Sophocles is supposed to have founded these.

What Euripides encountered was a convention and a tradition in which a form had been created as outlet for elementally passionate outbursts. He made little effort to alter this form. It provided for a chorus and principals. They wore masks, but not with the frozen grimaces that have come down to us from a later age. The masks were made of clinging materials, to which real hair and real beards were attached. They concealed the actual individuals, without depriving them of their humanity, as we can see in contemporary sculptures of them by Phidias. They enhanced the personality, they did not abstract it.

The costumes they wore were a little more formal than those of the audience. A god would appear bearing the symbols that were associated with him. Whenever there is splendor, Euripides dramatized it. On the other hand, when Euripides introduced a character who is poverty-stricken, he has him wear tatters. This innovation was initially chalked up against him, but, after he started the practice, Sophocles, who was not scandalized by it, followed it in his *Philoctetes* and his *Oedipus at Colonus*.

The established convention prescribed the number of choristers and actors permissible. This was hardly tampered with for a hundred years. Originally, there was only one actor, a "hypocrites," which means "answerer" or "responder," who stepped forward out of the chorus. Aeschylus supplemented him with a second principal speaker. By doing so, he introduced the intellectual element of dialogue into the tragedy. Subsequently, following the example of Sophocles, he provided for a third speaker. Ultimately, both he and Euripides occasionally introduced a fourth.

The wearing of masks permitted each speaking actor to play several parts, so that the cast of characters could actually be enlarged. There were eleven in *The Phoenician Maidens*. But in Euripides the typical grouping was composed of three characters, who would engage in "trialogue." Assigned parts as though engaged in a trial, they would act as the plaintiff, the defendant, and the judge. Convention forbade a greater variety of characters. It prescribed a certain degree of summation so that those who appeared would always represent the varieties of human nature. There were types who were immediately recognizable by their costumes, such as the very old man, the prophet, usually blind, the bearded mature man, the old woman, the mature matron, the youthful maiden, the young man, and others. It was of the nature of classical tragedy to evolve the individual out of the type. Euripides was a master of this art.

The chorus, which is such a great obstacle to viable production on the stage today, was taken for granted by the Hellenic tragedians. Aeschylus began by using twelve choristers, but an increase to fifteen was accepted by the audience. No doubt this was considered consistent when the number of the speaking actors was increased. The unerring Hellenic sense of proportion required it.

The choral passages stand in an obvious relation of importance to the length of the spoken test, largely because they are tied to it by the musical score. The chorus reveals the derivation of tragedy from religious ritual, but even in the earliest extant tragedies the chorus no longer acts out the religious ritual. They say nothing to remind the audience of the god, or that they had emerged from the circle of devotees who worshipped him.

It is equally easy to refute the assertion that the chorus is really the voice of the audience or the voice of the dramatist. In the work of Euripides the chorus is not always as dramatic as in the dramas of Aeschylus, which are named after his choruses, such as *The Persians*, *The Suppliant Women*, or *The Eumenides*, but even where, as notably in Euripides's later plays, he has the chorus specifically maintain its neutrality in the plot, this very neutrality achieves a dramatic purpose by displaying detachment from the proceedings.

Unfortunately we can have only the vaguest conception for ourselves of the chorus in action. Our knowledge of the Athenian theater is too meager. The use of sung recitative is among the very few alterations that Euripides made in the established convention, that is to say, the recitatives and arias of the soloists. Sophocles developed the form of antiphonal song between one or two soloists and the chorus to a high point of artistry. Euripides, however, by varying the verse meters succeeded in integrating the elements of the script. In this way the high art developed by Sophocles fell into disuse.

There are many long passages in Euripides's plays in which no words are spoken for long stretches of time; since everything is sung, it can rightly be called an opera. But Euripidean tragedy is a composite art work in which dance and mimic gesture are just as expressive and significant as words and music. These elements are capable of being performed separately, so that every scene has its separate and special character. They can also be projected simultaneously, so that they combine in one overall composition that culminates in effective theater.

The operatic devices of "stretto" and "finale" play a part in almost every one of the tragedies. Euripides liked to handle his prologues as overtures. The convention allowed the Athenian dramatist to synthesize logos (dialogue) and pathos (the most expressive height of musical impact) into a structural whole and compose them in a variety of forms.

There was another predilection of Euripides in his later tragedies within the convention that must be considered as characteristic as his elaboration of the musical score. He wrote the longest stichomythias, or serial dialogues, that we know. Stichomythia is a form of dialogue which is engaged in by a pair. The dramatist has to fill out the trimeter or the tetrameter of every verse. This calls for extreme inventive ingenuity. Stichomythia is an excellent contrivance for giving voice to a conflict or a quarrel. Each speaker opposes the argument of the other, point by point, insult for insult, in laconic expressiveness.

The tragic dramatists learned early to cultivate this form of dialogue into an instrument of art by which, for instance, the reports of messengers were made highly dramatic. They were required to answer inquiries and supply information in detail, one point at a time. Euripides was a great virtuoso when it came to stichomythia. He raised the stichomythia itself to the point of expressing the highest power of agitation by his technical skill. His success with it is an example of a distinguishing characteristic in the development of form, as the constantly advancing elasticity of the medium of expression always transcends the bounds of the strictly preserved stylization of the conventional form.

At the end, the basic artistic form was handled with such dexterity that it approaches the naturalness of the self-evident. The almost operatic passages of Sophocles and Euripides remind one of Mozartian finales. We find in both of them passages of dialogue that sound like ordinary conversation and were no doubt read accordingly. One must not deceive oneself, however, by supposing that this apparent simplicity is not a product of the highest art.

No sonorous instrumental orchestral accompaniment was necessary in the inexplicably fine acoustical properties of the Hellenic theater. Even today, a listener in the seventieth tier can understand every word normally spoken on the stage. A few instruments played by soloists were sufficient. A flute player came in at the head of the chorus and took his stand somewhere at the edge of the performing area to accompany them. In general, one can say that the flute provided the dionysian element in the music, while string instruments, such as the lyre and the cythera, expressed the apollonian elements. In addition, there was a percussion section, containing instruments like drums (the tympani, the cymbals) and a kind of castanets (crotales), which also, to be sure, reflected dionysian elements.

The music theory of the Hellenes comprised not only variations in the tonal modes, melody, rhythm, tempo, and dynamic, but it also ascribed moral qualities to instruments that expressed their meaning symbolically when they appeared in the ensemble. The flute, for instance, was regarded as having an emotional, even an orgiastic, voice. If a flute player preceded a chorus, this alone could signify a certain foreignness if he wore an oriental costume.

It is evident that Euripides favored such foreign elements in his later plays. In his texts the adjective barbarian was employed unlike the way we use it; it meant only "non-Hellenic." In any case, Euripides did not share the customary Hellenic disdain for the "barbarian." In his favoring of "barbarian" elements is reflected the movement in contemporary music that was branded "modern" and was far in advance of the century in which the tragedies were written. It was vehemently rejected by the conservatives.

The extreme stylization of the convention of the theater required that the gait and the gestures of the actors closely conform to dancelike rhythmic patterns whenever musical accompaniment was provided.

Rhythm and melody supported the action, the emotion might be raised to the highest degree of exaltation, yet the representation of truth remained restricted by strict rules. Every choral passage had its individual choreography, but this was not in any way similar to our ballet or interpretative dances. The dancing manifested its derivation from religious ritual. It employed highly conventional forms and relied on the complete mastery acquired by every member of the chorus over the traditionally required movements.

Lament had its specified gestures, as did joy or horror. The movements handed down by tradition heightened the spontaneity of the sentiments depicted, rather than hindering it. This can be observed even today in any southern country. A funeral dirge also had its own traditional ritual and choreography.

Yet the variations possible in choreography within the prescribed convention were endlessly rich. This is shown by the complex strophic forms of the choral songs. Poetry was conceived by the dramatist as a form of song. Poets were their own composers. As they were usually their own stage directors as well, they provided also the choreography. They heard and saw their texts in their minds as spoken, sung, and danced.

We know practically nothing about their kind of music. This hinders us in trying to picture for ourselves the dancelike patterns they created. We can only guess at approximate analogies from the folk dances preserved in remote regions of Greece. I refer not to those slicked up into conscious folklore, but to dances like those Béla Bartók gathered in his research on primitive folk music in the Balkans. In a different direction, we might also call to mind the highly stylized dance forms of the Asiatic theater, for example, the East Indian Kathakali or especially the Japanese No, since both of these were aspects of theater. Their theater, like the Greek theater, is a combination of several arts in the same framework.

Even the hero's solo part, as Euripides preferred to write it, had something dancelike in it. In the Athenian theater it was considered a very admirable exercise of high art in an actor if he combined the bearing and gesture required by the spoken text with the dance movements and song of the musical score. As the verse itself had to conform to traditional stylization in its strict observance of form and organization of dialogue, the music could easily flow into bodily movement to heighten the impression made by the text.

Certainly, in the beginnings of tragedy, this stylization was stamped with the frozen attitudes we know in the sculpture of the same period. In the later period of antiquity the deportment became freer. We have already noted that Aeschylus and Sophocles demanded that the actor project the same human truth that their contemporaries, the great sculptors, set as the goal of their art. Stylization was the point of departure for study and rehearsal, not its consequence. The actor was required to individualize the character in each role, within the traditional conventional forms, and convey the true personality with the sharpest possible clarity, to express the spirit of the sentiment prescribed by the text with dramatic spontaneity. It has been attested that the border had not only been touched but transgressed in either the earlier or the later centuries. But the texts required, nevertheless, that the acting in even such passages of madness and fury must conform to the musical and dance styles prescribed.

Euripides pushed formal conventions almost to the breaking point by freighting them with a content they could only bear by means of his virtuosity. But this span—here concentrated truth, there highly stylized convention—was the essence of the art of acting in the tragic theater. In its greatest moments it must have inspired the same reactions we experience today when we see the sculpture of the same period, such as the bronze Poseidon in the National Museum in Athens, the caryatid maidens of the Erechtheum, or the figures at Olympia: form as the concentrated expression of truth.

Seventeen thousand spectators attended the performances. The theater was probably always full to capacity. The seating area, somewhat wider than a semicircle, rising in tiers like an amphitheater, nearly surrounded a circular space at the bottom, set aside primarily for the chorus. It was also the space for dancing. In Greek the word "orchestra" means the place for dancing.

Tangent to one side of this circle was the "skene," a podium or platform reached by two or three easy steps. By the time of Euripides this platform of stone had already been constructed. At some point it was decided to use stone or building material for the entire theater, but this process was not completed until a hundred years later, in about the year 330. This basic podium, or stage, probably had wings protruding from both its sides, the "paraskenia." Behind the skene a grove of trees extended down toward the valley behind it. The fluttering leaves on the olive trees made the slope down toward the shore look like silver, a play of color that, with the blue of the sea and the azure of the sky, united in an indescribable harmony. In the clear light of Athens the characters moving about on the stage must have seemed closer to the spectators than they would on any other stage in the world.

A temporary structure was erected on the stage for each day of the festival. We do, however, have plays of a later period that could be presented on the bare stage without special background. There were several typical structures available. By the time of Euripides the background most frequently put up was the façade of a palace with protruding wings. Later this was to be made of stone and was to become the permanent stage. But in two of Euripides's surviving plays he called for simple houses. In *Electra* it is actually a peasant's hut. In three plays he specifies a temple. In his *Ion* he has a pillared temple with a pediment, around a sanctuary. Most probably the carpenters copied the façade of the famous temple of Apollo at Delphi and made it look like the original. For *The Suppliant Women* the entrance to the sanctuary at Eleusis was probably copied. The structures were of wood and could be painted in colors. None of Euripides's plays required painting an outdoor landscape for a backdrop.

In three plays he requires a tent encampment, with one large tent, one of medium size, and two at the sides. Access was up a few steps that could be erected on top of the stone podium. One of the satyr plays calls for a cave, which could also be used for other purposes.

On the festival day one play was given in the forenoon, and the other three after the intermission required by the midday heat. It was only possible to erect a complete change of scene between the first and the second plays. Euripides never required a change of scene within a play, although Aeschylus and Sophocles did occasionally.

Sometimes even a typical scene would carry a characteristic or dramatic note. A palace could display oriental splendor, as in *Helen*, which is played in Egypt, or archaic antiquity, as in the Theban palace of Pentheus in *The Bacchae*. Medea's home was a refugee lodge. In *The Trojan Women* the tents of the women collected from Troy as slaves looked different from those of Agamemnon, who was the commander-in-chief of the Hellenes. The temple of Iphigenia among the Taurians was exotic and barbarian. The temple of Ion evoked the aura of Delphi through a long opening scene of words and music.

Every stage setting was merely a background for the theatrical action. Characters could stand on the roof of a palace. In *The Phoenician Maidens* a charming young girl climbs up with an elderly servant. He names the troop units of an army he points out to her as they approach the city below. In another play, *Orestes*, a similarly very young girl is dragged to the roof by assassins while the flame and smoke of torches rise from inside the palace.

The platform which we have spoken of earlier, could be rolled out on wheels through the great central gate of the palace or temple. In *Heracles*, we see Heracles raving on such a platform, roped to a column on it, surrounded by his loved ones whom he has slain. Sick characters could be rolled out onto the stage on stretchers. Corpses could be borne on biers in a solemn funeral procession. Several such processions (called a "pompe") are in the stage directions Euripides wrote.

Kings or generals usually appeared with their bodyguards. The top command would be identified by such an escort. In *Electra* Orestes and Pylades, with their servants, come on the scene clothed in inconspicuous travel garb. In *The Suppliant Women* the mothers come on in a long procession. In *The Trojan Women* the women are driven like cattle onto the ships in a long gruesome parade, and Andromache rides in on a cart atop a pile of war booty, herself a prize of war, with her child in her arms. In *Iphigenia in Aulis*, Clytemnestra, magnificently gowned, along with Iphigenia, comes on stage riding on a chariot drawn by horses when they arrive in Aulis. Later, in *Electra*, Clytemnestra enters in an ostentatious royal chariot when she approaches the hut her daughter lives in.

In all the tragedies, stage groupings were arranged to heighten their dramatic effect on the audience and to leave indelible impressions on their memories. Many of them are not indicated in the text. They can only be inferred. Written stage directions were not required because the dramatists were generally their own stage directors.

For the plays of Euripides, one piece of stage apparatus was essential. This was the "machina," a crane carrying a gondola that could be swung over the stage. It was also called a "theologeion," because the god within it spoke down to the humans on the stage. Athena appeared in it, radiant, with her spear and her aegis, as did Apollo, Artemis, and Aphrodite. The gondola would be adorned with the sacred symbols by which each god or goddess could be recognized. This was worked out with the same careful attention to detail as were the statues of the gods in their temples. The gondola could also be built to represent a chariot or a flying vehicle. The dragon-drawn chariot in which Medea flies off through the air is such a gondola.

This brings us to the much debated and maligned "deus ex machina" itself. We cannot discuss it without asking ourselves what Euripides intended its purpose and function to serve in his tragedies.

This requires us to penetrate from the externals of the stage into the inner meaning of the play. We cannot explore the significance of the deus ex machina without first establishing what the gods altogether meant to Euripides. Were gods to him only a variety of humans, as is stated in one of the tragedies? Would they have been gods without humans to worship them? Or, to turn the question around, were there people who had no gods? Were there gods at all?

What are humans like, whether they believe in the gods or only pretend to, like Pericles? What are people like if they really do not believe in them at all and act as if there were no powers above mankind?

GODS, HEROES, MEN

It has always been within the province of the theater to delineate the invisible. Realism in the theater is a later development. Witches and ghosts were still appearing on the stage in Shakespeare's theater. Today we realize that audiences do not necessarily have to believe in supernatural beings to concede to them theatrical reality. Even Brecht had gods and angels appear on his stage. They may be merely symbols or portents. Or, they can express what others believe, though this is not necessarily what the dramatist himself believes in. When a dramatist has gods appear in his plays, it does not in the least signify that he believes in them himself.

Gods appear more frequently in the plays of Euripides than they do in those of Aeschylus or Sophocles. Ever since Horace, observers have charged that Euripides's device of having a god appear ex machina at the last minute, at the point at which everything was hopelessly tangled, or nothing but the most horrible consequences seemed possible, was a method of relying on a much too convenient convention to provide a solution to the dilemma he had got himself into, that he himself was unable to resolve.

There's something to this if it is formulated as Goethe did: "The insoluble dilemma is as it were shunted aside by a miracle in Euripides," that is, by a miracle in which no one has to believe. Euripides releases his public from the world he has unfolded before them. They realize it was all only theater. Why should the illusion of the myth be destroyed, even if we do not believe in the myth any longer? Thinking people will understand what is meant.

Even before Euripides, Sophocles was a master in the use of such irony, handling it all with great smoothness. Euripides made irony the main element in all his presentations. He seems to be perpetually calling out to the spectators: "Nothing is what it appears to be. Do not believe anything I let these people on the stage say to you. They may be deceiving you or only themselves. What you are being told about men in times past may possibly be true, but we know it only by men."

In Hellenic tragedy, the attention of the audience was not focused on "what" was taking place on the stage. Everyone knew these stories from childhood. They were more interested in how they were being presented in the dramatist's version of the motivations, his exposition of their significance, in the fresh light he brings to the old familiar stories. For this reason the gods were only statements of mythical facts that the dramatist added to the report he was submitting. They might have existed, but what if they did not? What of it if the legendary characters were only men who tried to take advantage of the good repute of a god to cover up their shameful deeds? What if there were, indeed, gods but gods who were quite other than people believed them to be?

The Hellenes had no class of professional priests except for their seers or prophets. Religious observances were performed by municipal officials and citizens of distinction. They were regarded as a function of the polis, hence political in their nature. In all the plays of Euripides there are only prophets. Their business was to forecast the future, by the stars, or by the flight of birds, or by the appearance of the entrails of animals slaughtered as sacrifices.

Their greatest power lay in the pronouncing of oracles. Even in late antiquity, people from great distances, including Roman emperors, made pilgrimages to Delphi, where the pythoness, seated on her tripod, in a trance induced by the mists arising from the local subterranean springs, babbled her mystic utterances.

Anyone who had gone to Delphi—whatever else he might have thought—could not avoid receiving the impression that this was sacred soil, that this spot was a place distinguished above all others in heaven or on earth. But the gnomic words of the prophetess always had to be interpreted by priests, according to the formula. The ambiguity of their interpretations was famous. The oracle predicted to King Croesus: "If you cross the river, you will destroy a great empire." It turned out the empire he destroyed was his own.

Even today men share a wish to look into the future. Whoever can profess to gratify it can count on our ineradicable belief that there are unknown powers both in and out of the world. It was this belief that gave Delphi such potency. When the Hellenes began to devise constitutions for their states, they called on priests from Delphi to give them sanction. This procedure was not merely ceremonial. Even today we require public officials to swear an oath of office when they are inaugurated. The temple at Delphi was a political factor of considerable importance.

But quite early, suspicions began to be aroused that the priests manipulated the utterances of Pythia when they offered interpretations. They were suspected of being open to bribery. Belief in the oracle itself remained unshaken, but suspicion was attached to those who translated the mystic expressions into understandable language. A similar situation existed in every city in the fifth century B.C. The seers who practiced prophecy as a profession, were officials of the polis. They were asked for interpretations of omens, but people were not always prepared to accept them confidently without some further verification.

It stands to reason that belief in divination was far more widespread among the common people than among the intellectuals. But in a democracy it is the majority who control. As the majority believed in the powers of prophets, the polis had to consult them officially. They were consulted before the ruinous invasion of Sicily began. Thucydides reports that after the disaster, all the diviners, the readers of omens, everyone who had professed to be inspired by the gods in their forecasts, were called to account. Obviously, all the forecasters had been manipulated by the war party. And that was in 413 B.C.!

By the time of Sophocles and Euripides, doubt had

begun to undermine belief in these soothsayers, but confidence still persisted in the trustworthiness of the extremely aged blind, who were supposed to be able to "see" more than ordinary mortals. Tiresias knows more than Creon or Oedipus, not because he can read the intentions of the gods better, but because he has known the world and man. He is truly wise. In *The Bacchae*, Euripides provides this old blind man with hair-splitting arguments. He can debate like a trained sophist. On the other hand, Calchas, the prophet consulted about the Trojan War, who does not appear in person in any of the plays that have survived, is a thoroughly corrupt evil character and a political "wire-puller." It becomes evident that a "seer" could be influenced to see better in one direction than in another.

It was the same with gods. They represent not what the dramatist believes, but what the audience believes. They have value, not only to the characters of the play in which they appear or reveal themselves, but even more to the audience, which knows perfectly well that human actors are concealed behind the masks of the gods.

Athena appears in three of Euripides's plays. Most people believed in her either as the patron goddess for whom Athens was named, or in the way Pericles did, who ordered her statue carved as a symbol. Her temple, the Parthenon, stood for the splendor of the polis. It is understandable that Euripides gives her the last word in *The Suppliant Women*, his most political play as well as the one that praises Athens the most eloquently. In the other two plays in the finales of which she appears, *Iphigenia in Aulis* and *Ion*, she is not only the goddess ex machina who "shunts the insoluble dilemma aside" in order to make the plot conform with the myth but also the substitute for other gods who cannot or do not wish to appear because they have caused such dreadful havoc with predictions that were followed as directives.

The deus ex machina can therefore fulfill an ironic function. It is possible that the pretense of his intrusion fills both the characters on the stage and the audience with the same sense of bitterness. They all charge the god with responsibility for what has happened.

Apollo appears in this light, at the end of *Orestes*, as the dreadfully guilty party on whose conscience the murder of Clytemnestra, and all its consequences, must rest. Even those who believe in the gods must admit that they are unjust, cruel, and inexplicable. Should one revere such gods? Yes. But only as one of their victims expresses it: "Oh Zeus, I beseech you, whoever you may be, you who have founded the world and sit upon its throne, who are incomprehensible to us, whether from the course of events or in the understanding of mankind!"

The "course of events" and the "understanding of mankind" are philosophic concepts of the Hellenes that relate to their theories of explaining divinity. The former includes the ideas of inevitability, compulsion, and necessity that govern the real world of nature (the "physis"). The latter is "nus," the spirit, the power of thought. Anaxagoras said that nus is god or god is nus. For this opinion his contemporaries in Athens forced him to defend himself in a prosecution.

Is it Euripides who speaks this prayer to Zeus? No, it is Hecuba, the regal slave, the victim of the gods, who clings to the last possibility, which is to faith. Euripides let her have the philosophy of the existence of a regulating supreme power or of an all-directing world spirit to show it against the backdrop of the actual realities of existence, as illustrated by Hecuba's plight as victim of the gods. Needless to say, her devout prayer for the execution of Helen remains unheeded.

If there are gods, they are beyond good and evil. If they give us the gift of the good, the beautiful, and the admirable, as for example in art and in the theater, such beauty is always one side of a coin of which the reverse is the frightful. It is only in this sense that we can understand the god Dionysus in *The Bacchae.* Some say that Euripides, facing his own death, begged Dionysus for forgiveness for what he had charged the gods with in his earlier plays. What does this conversion signify? In Dionysus he embodies what the gods represent, if indeed there are gods—that is, the ambivalence, the antimony of their acts.

Dionysus comes to Thebes because this land of his birth refuses to acknowledge his divinity. He displays his power by converting the women into bacchantes and the old men into senile fools. He is indignant about the young king, Pentheus, who rejects him and who suspects sexual excesses in the Dionysian orgies. So what does he do to manifest his power over this disbeliever? He incites the sex instinct innate in human nature to the point of lasciviousness, which deprives man of his senses. In marvelous verses Euripides depicts the serenity and modesty with which the bacchantes behave under the trees on the mountain once they have exhausted their orgy of ecstasy and torn apart the animals, their victims, with their hands and teeth.

This lovely tranquility is the other side of Dionysus, the bringer of blessings. What is it then that makes the women forsake their modest deportment when they discern a man lurking in hiding and spying on them? It is simply the wilderness lurking in man's hearts, the wolfish instinct that makes animals of them and drives them to treat others as cattle.

Dionysus is the latent terror that is a born ingredient of the human constitution. Woe to us when it is awakened! The scene in which the mother, in triumphant fury, brings her son's head impaled on a stake onto the stage is the most gruesome theater ever devised. Such is the working of Dionysus. It is also his work when the most horrible is presented as a form of beauty more pure than is any other of the creations of Euripides.

In form *The Bacchae* is Euripides's most austere play. But this austerity is more than a mere harking back to the ancient, the primitive, the archaic principle of tragedy. It is the product of dramatic skill, the medium with which he harnesses the horror and carves it, so to speak, in living stone. He conveys the sense of beauty not as the beginning of the hideous but as its ending.

And this is what gods may be like. They may also be no more than pictures attached to names of ideas. Euripides created many such personifications. But that is typical of the Hellenic spirit. As early as Aeschylus, Dike (justice) became in his mind only an idea in the spirit of the word itself, a picture of the concept. In his play it is Kratos (power) and Bie (force) that bind Prometheus in fetters. Similarly Euripides makes gods of Lype (sorrow) and Phthonos (envy). He identifies Zeus with Nus (reason) to remind us of the contrast between the goddesses Isotes (equality) and Philotimia (thirst for glory) in *The Phoenician Maidens*.

Sophocles conceived the gods as the powers that motivate human actions. After him, Euripides set up Aphrodite (Cypris) as a moving force. In unhappy Phaedra she demonstrated the dominion she exercises over humans. There is no instance of happiness in love in any of the Hellenic tragedies that have come down to us. After long separation, a man and a woman can sink into each other's arms, but it is only as if they were brother and sister. Frustrated love converts itself into hate. Aphrodite becomes the embodiment of both desire and horror.

In one play two demonic witchlike creatures appear. One of them, Lyssa, speaks as from the depths, with a serpent's glassy eye; the other, Iris, the sister of the Harpies, flutters her opalescent wings in the machina. Both predict that something unspeakably dreadful will happen, that the sinister and the dread will spread. On the other hand, on two occasions, two other spirits, the Dioscuri, appear in verses as bright as starlight. They are the protectors of ships and sailors.

Euripides always liked to present gods symbolically in pairs in his prologues, e.g., Apollo and Thanatos (life and death), or Aphrodite and Artemis (desire and chastity) or Poseidon and Athena. Poseidon and Athena, who appear in the prologue to *The Trojan Women*, oppose each other in homeric myth. Each espoused opposing sides in the Trojan War, but now they are united to punish the Hellenes, who must do penance for the outrages they have perpetrated in Troy. This alliance is not limited to the prologue, the function of which is to cast light on all the events that follow in the course of the play. Here, the two gods make an appeal to the audience that cannot be misunderstood. Poseidon and Athena were equally the patron divinities of the polis Athens. Poseidon personified the sea, on which the power and wealth of Athens were founded, so the spectators realized at once that Troy in the play symbolized nothing other than Athens.

Some critics have charged that this prologue is lacking in artistic skill, because the speakers, some of whom are mortal beings, make statements that anticipate the exposition section of the play in which organically they belong. But for a theater that possessed no curtain to separate the stage from the audience, and which had the actors appear in the so-called proagon ceremony before the play began in order to introduce themselves to the audience, there was little need to adhere to the technique of exposition—no more so than there was for the theater of Brecht, in which such prologues are frequent.

Just as the deus ex machina can shunt the insoluble dilemma to one side, so the prologue can take the place of an exposition section and tell what needs to be told before the action of the play itself begins. After such an opening, the play begins in earnest, when the myth ends and the actions are those of humans.

To make them human heroes, the heroes of the myths must first be deprived of their mythological character. This is principally what shocked the audience about the plays of Euripides. Euripides was accused of disparaging the traditional heroes. It is correct that he refused to pay attention to ideas that had endeared themselves to people if he considered them wrong or even based on lies. Hellas's beloved treasures meant little to him as he was after what he considered the truth. On the contrary, he felt he must drag heroes down to earth from the radiance in which their mythological immortality bathed them. His goal was not to destroy them but only to reduce their stature. Other legendary characters were raised from the dust if in his view they had been denigrated without being truly at fault.

Euripides refused to allow figures whom he brought onto the stage to be glorified in the golden aura of the good old days, which were, in fact, irretrievably gone. He was not interested in showing people who would be, at best, the stuff dreams are made of. He would present them within the framework of the convention, not destroying but, at most, merely enlarging the frame. This stylization signified concentration, abbreviation, and transference into his own time rather than remoteness, sublimity, or archaism.

It was a theater that did not present the present time, but nevertheless reflected it. He transmuted the old myths into episodes of his own time by the power of his imagination. He brought the old characters so completely into his own time that they might be taking part in events that were happening currently. He asked himself how these events would be happening if they were occurring today. What motives would impel these men if they were living today? To achieve this is the secret of true genius.

About 421 B.C. Euripides offered *The Suppliant Women*, a play that demanded of his contemporaries that they have confidence at least in the possibility of improving things even if there was little likelihood of the good ever being attained. In his later plays, as he became increasingly embittered, there is one theme that always comes to the fore: he tried to make vivid the fact that appearance meant just as much in the old myths as it did in his time. In both the past and in Euripides's time, reality, in contradistinction to appearance, had almost lost meaning.

The tragic dramatists knew the abysses of the human soul so well that Sigmund Freud named one of his most profound psychological discoveries the oedipus complex. Euripides also showed, by the example of Phaedra, how the inextricable enmeshment of erotic feeling with social standing can provoke a woman in love even to precipitate murder. This woman, driven to despair and suicide by her unrequited passion for her stepson is capable of causing the death of her beloved not because she hates him now, but because, after a dreadful scene for which she is only partly responsible, she is terrified that her husband may learn of her infatuation. She takes her life, but to save her reputation, to preserve the image she wishes her survivors and the next world to keep of her, she slanders an innocent man even against her own better judgment.

All later writers who utilized this story, which Euripides may have actually invented, felt the way Phaedra made the false accusation (by means of a letter she ties to her arm before killing herself) to be so monstrous that it does not appear in their adaptations.

Nevertheless, for all that, it lost none of its horrible truth.

Euripides's plays constantly deride men who strive for riches. They cannot take any of the glittering stuff with them into the grave. Power, too, appears, as it does in Shakespeare, only as pomp that can collapse in a day. What, then, is hidden behind the masks of the gods above, when we try to see through them, today as well as then?

Let us look, for example, at the great Agamemnon, the commander-in-chief of the Hellenic forces in the Trojan War, who is compelled by a prophet's forecast to agree to sacrifice his oldest daughter to placate the angry goddess, so that she will grant the favoring wind needed to speed on their way the ships becalmed in the harbor at Aulis. This prophetic admonition might have been manipulated. Calchas, the seer, could have made a pact with Odysseus, who was not favorable to Agamemnon. But that is immaterial. What matters is that his utterances were believed by the crowd. Consequently, the whole army was seized with a kind of mass hysteria. To their minds, Troy was another Sicily, a place to be plundered. They could hardly expect Troy willingly to surrender its wealth and riches without a fight, not to mention the women they were greedy to capture. They wanted to get started.

So the all-powerful Agamemnon finds himself compelled to placate his army when his wife and daughter arrive in camp. If good politics consists in drawing the right conclusions from a correctly assessed situation, he proves himself an excellent politician. He reconciles himself to what he sees is inevitable. He knows the army would not permit the women to be sent home again. If he were to do that and accompany them, his soldiers would follow him and seek in his own country the booty they were promised if they conquered Troy. The mob threatens to revolt just before the time set for the sacrifice. Thus Iphigenia is sent to the block.

What is this called? It is practical politics. Shamefully one keeps silent when confronted with the logic of hard facts. Agamemnon knows that. I am the slave of the mob, he laments. But later the myth will be: I acted in the best interest of the nation. It is those who would tear down this cloak of illusion who are the subverters, the villains who are lacking in love of their own country.

But does this play not glorify the sacrifice of one's own life for one's country and project it with passionate emotion? Yes. Iphigenia tears through the net in which practical politics has enmeshed her. She announces in a wonderful speech that she goes to her death freely and joyfully in order to save her fatherland. Her fatherland? Yes. That is how the text reads, but we have seen what the actual facts are. Only a human being who has not yet learned to know the world and its ways could still believe in the delusions in which history has veiled the true aims of practical politics.

In Euripides there are three such heroic young people, in addition to Iphigenia. There are two maidens —Macaria, in *Children of Heracles*, Polyxena, in *Hecuba*—and one young boy, Menoeceus, in *The Phoenician Maidens*. Euripides does not hesitate to devote his most charming verses to their death-defying courage. At least, fame will be their lot, even if their sacrifice proves to be worthless. How lovely would the world be if reality were such as these young idealists visualize it to be.

The culmination of these themes is to be seen in the manner in which Euripides presents war on his stage. Many plays revolve around it. *The Trojan Women* contains his most striking statement. It is not enough for peace lovers to wail and groan. The writer must reveal the real motives for which thousands are urged to lay down their lives. *The Trojan Women* discloses these in the shameful conduct of the victors. They stop at nothing, not at the violation of young priestesses at their altars, not at the destruction of a young child who is to be slain at the ruins of the walls of Troy. Even this execution is excused by their "practical" politics.

But the hand of Euripides was revealed even more openly in another instance. He decided to make the Athenians a gift of a pretty fable, his *Helen*, when he composed a new play after the Sicilian disaster. The masses who do not wish to think would get joy out of it, and possibly also a little comfort. The others were given to think as follows: In truth, Helen was not abducted by Paris. Hera sent a phantom to Troy to replace Helen. Helen herself was actually transported through the air to Egypt, there modestly to await her husband, Menelaus, who would return to fetch her home again. "All for Helen!" had been a war cry for the Hellenes. Now they would find out it meant really: "All for a phantom!" The story of the theft of Helen was used to obscure the real reason for the war, which was in fact nothing but a war of conquest. How much can be accomplished in this world by illusion! Would Helen be judged in the future for the deeds committed in her name? Or in the name of the illusion of her presence in Troy? Or in the name of the actual truth which nobody knows? Needless to say, the beautiful Helen will remain for all time the cause of the great war. So many tears have been shed over her abduction.

Men are driven through this life not only by the incomprehensibly arbitrary will of the gods, or by ineluctable fate, but as much, or even more, by their own delusions, by their self-deception, by their ill-disguised appetites, by their greed for possessions or for power or glory. This is why, as in *Ion*, they are catapulted hither and yon, from good fortune to ill and back again to good. Even the great are only men. If they are wise they yearn for the happiness of the ordinary man, as do Agamemnon and Orestes. But can the simple man achieve happiness in a world ruled by the great who have the power to offer him up as a sacrifice? The simple man is blinded by the glamor of the great, but if he is clever he will shake his head and say to himself: Why should I covet something I might lose? Something I will lose one of these days, in any case.

Such are the people Euripides drives over his stage, pitilessly but sympathetically. Do they grow in awareness with maturity? Maybe some do. Others grow great through suffering, but more, so many, are pitifully ludicrous even at the edge of the grave. The endearing, transfigured young people in his casts stand side by side with the living corpses (the dying Alcestis, Alcmene who survives all trials), the wasted bodies of the starving (like Phaedra or Orestes), the blind, ruined Oedipus. To all these we must also add the barbarian women, wild and untamed, but often more human than the Hellenes! It is a long cavalcade of characters, a long parade of humanity.

Whatever may have been charged against him, or may still be, Euripides was a great dramatist. Goethe said of him, a year before his own death, "All who would deny the loftiness of his work are little creatures, not capable of such elevated sentiments, or unashamed mountebanks who by their presumptiousness tried to make themselves out more noteworthy than they truly are." And at the end of the same year, he wrote in his diary: "Have the nations of the world produced a dramatist since Euripides who is worthy even to hand him his carpet slippers?"

Aristotle called the theater of Euripides the most tragic of all. It has the dignity of a noble style and the beauty of structure in the grand manner. It is a theater without belief, without hope, without mercy. Dignity is only where there is truth.

There is nothing here for sheltered Christians, for Marxists, for existentialists. It is great theater, theater such as has never again been written.

PLAYS

Alcestis

Apollo has served out a term as a shepherd for King Admetus of Thessaly. This was decreed by his father Zeus as a punishment for disobedience. To reward the king for his generous hospitality, Apollo gets the Moirae, the goddesses of destiny and death, to agree that Admetus can postpone death so long as he can get someone to die in his place. After all those to whom he has turned, including his old parents, refuse to sacrifice themselves for him, his wife, Alcestis, declares she is ready to do so. His death, however, was not then actually impending.

Years of relative happiness have passed for them, but now Admetus's time has come. Therefore, a mortal illness has stricken Alcestis. Her death is awaited from moment to moment.

Now a race begins between life and death. In the prologue appears Apollo, radiant from on high, as the god of the sun and of life. He bids Admetus farewell because he must not linger in the presence of Death. Thanatos, the black angel, the god of death, is already emerging from below. He and Apollo exchange bitter words. Why, Apollo asks, must he take the young when he gets all men sooner or later. Death says that robbing the young of life forces people to recognize his power. Apollo then accuses him of caring only for the gifts that accompany the dead, but Death insists that he treats the poor as he does the rich. In a burst of final anger, Apollo reveals that he knows that Death will lose this time.

Music swells up. A chorus of older citizens enters. The appointed day is passing rapidly, and so far no death lament can yet be heard from the manorhouse. A weeping maid comes out of the house to report to the chorus how things are going. Sullenly she satisfies their curiosity. Life has almost abandoned Alcestis. Her body is consumed with fever. She begs only to be allowed to see the light of the sun once more before the end.

The great doorway clanks open. A picture of misery, she is rolled out from the dark interior. The chorus weeps aloud. The dying woman staggers out onto the terrace, supported on her husband's arm. She is robed in the magnificent funeral costume in which her maids have prepared her for burial. Her two children try to clasp her. The women and servants of the court carry out the litter for the obsequies. All are weeping.

The music of the choral songs swells up into strong emotion. The lament of renunciation sounds forth. Trembling, Alcestis raises herself up, disturbed by a vision she sees. It is the oarsman Charon in his skiff, beckoning to her. He climbs on to the bank from his boat and approaches her. She puts out her arm to ward him off, but he seizes it. Now she feels she is about to be led away and laments her fate. She collapses and is laid on the bier. Admetus moans that he cannot bear to live on without her. But we know, whatever he says, that she is dying that he may live.

The music dies down. In the tense silence, Alcestis rouses herself. Leaning on her supporters, she gives her last message. Composed, almost drained of emotion, she yet speaks clearly. She addresses Admetus directly for the first time in the play. She had herself brought out because she wants witnesses to hear her last request to him. She tells Admetus that she has chosen death rather than live on without him. And then she asks one promise: that he not give her children another mother.

Admetus vows to obey her last wish. His protestations and endearments are so exaggerated that they make one suspicious. He vows that he will have an image of Alcestis made that he will always keep close to him, that he is renouncing all revelry and entertainment, that games or dancing will be forbidden in his home. With her will be buried all his joy in life.

Then he elaborates these pledges, piling one vow onto another. Like Orpheus, he will descend into the underworld and fetch her back again. But if that cannot be done, he will install their marriage bed down there. He is ready to lie down in her coffin and be interred with her. The dying Alcestis pays no attention to all this. She hands the children over to him, reminding them of what he has promised. When

Admetus throws himself down, embracing her, she tells him, almost smilingly, that time will heal his grief. Her last farewell is addressed only to her children.

Then Death enters, and Alcestis knows the time has come to leave life. The chorus sings the dirge. Now there is music again. Bowed down over the bier, her little son sings his farewell to his dying mother.

At once the grief-stricken Admetus rises to his full height, all king, in his majesty. He proclaims national mourning. The bier is carried into the home. He and the children follow it with their retinue. The great gateway to the manorhouse drops shut. The chorus intones a lament. The good name of Alcestis will light her way into the afterworld, and throughout Hellas the poets will sing of her. They add, pointedly, that the man lucky enough to be her husband would be free of sorrow all his life.

Now Heracles, the rescuer Apollo had foretold, approaches. From far off, Heracles, as he is shown in countless pictures, attired in his lion pelt and armed with his club, can be seen. He is still pledged to complete the labors that Hera requires of him. He is being punished because his adulterous father, Zeus, violated his marriage vow when he made love to Amphitryon's wife, Heracles's mother, in the guise of Amphitryon. Heracles calls out jovially to the chorus, who are absorbed in their lamentations. Now they turn to him. He inquires for Admetus, his friend.

Heracles explains that he only wishes to stop in for a visit on his way to more labors he must still perform. The commotion is heard inside the manorhouse.

The great door opens. The funeral cortege stands ready to set out in the dim light. Admetus steps out in a black cloak. When he see Heracles he is taken by surprise and put into a difficult situation. What is he to do? Famous for his hospitality, he cannot just turn his visitor away from his threshold. On the other hand, he cannot ask him to share his present grief.

This is the reason, as he explains later, why he kept the death of Alcestis secret from Heracles, telling him only that a relative died and must quickly be laid to rest. After that, he will return and entertain his guest with his customary hospitality. In the meantime the servants will be directed to serve him everything the kitchen and the cellar can offer. Heracles agrees, though suspecting all is not as it should be. He lets himself be conducted into the manorhouse.

But is not the true reason that Admetus is ashamed to confess the truth? How can he admit to this fearless hero, whom, as we all know, Death itself cannot frighten, that he has allowed his wife to die in his place?

This is how he begins to spin the web of deceit in which he will soon entangle himself.

The arrival of Heracles was the first untoward event. The second occurs when the cortege has just begun to cross the stage. The dirges have started. Admetus's aged father, King Pheres, though not invited, appears with his retinue, to take part in the burial. It becomes clear that there is deep discord between father and son. We soon learn why.

The bier is set down. Pheres pays his last respects to Alcestis. The words he uses are so chosen that they must inflame Admetus to white heat: he speaks of the debt Admetus owes to Alcestis for dying in his place, and he says he too is in her debt for saving the life of his son. When he prepares to touch the coffin, Admetus can no longer restrain his anger. The strife that ensues over the body rises to noisy vehemence that borders on the grotesque. It is thrillingly composed by Euripides to lead to the ghastly conclusion that Pheres closes the dispute with. Which is to say that he was not imbecile enough to die for Admetus, as Alcestis was.

This altercation serves to unmask Admetus, but it is the master hand of Euripides that leads him to accomplish his own unmasking. Admetus works himself up into a raging fury. He shoves his father's servants aside, away from the coffin. He tears the wreaths out of their hands and stamps them underfoot. He erupts into insensate hatred, denying that Pheres is his father. He cannot restrain his bitterness that his father, with only a few years to live, had refused to die in his place.

To this Pheres responds that God's sunshine is a sweet thing. He says that he has given Admetus life and power, but that he is no more bound to die for Admetus than Admetus is to die for him. How can a man so base as to accept his wife's sacrifice accuse other people of being mean-spirited?

Admetus orders him to leave. Pheres turns to go off with his retinue, but he flings back the taunt that Admetus is the murderer of his wife. A paralyzing silence follows. Then Admetus pulls himself together. He orders that the cortege proceed. The coffin is lifted high. Torches light the way for it. The chorus follows it with the ritual song of burial. The stage is empty.

Now comic action follows the grotesque. Noise issues from the manorhouse. The door is thrown open. A huge man emerges roaring. Heracles is behaving at his worst. He has been conducting himself like a highwayman, a crass ruffian, acting as if he were in a saloon. Yet in fact, he is in a house in mourning. He staggers out with a heavy beaker in his hand, a myrtle wreath on his head, reeling and babbling. The tenor of his words is, eat, drink, and be merry, for tomorrow you die.

And then the truth is revealed to him. The servant discloses it in spite of Admetus's orders. Heracles fumes. He was deceived. He grabs and shakes the poor devil of a servant, who runs away from him. This makes Heracles rise to his most untamed greatness. He has been treated like a barbarian. His host might have been acting with the best intentions, with hospitality to Heracles in mind, but even courtesy can be carried too far. The shame he has been permitted to perpetrate on the memory of the dead can only be wiped away by the most heroic deed. He rushes off to the grave.

The stage is empty again. In a short while we see the funeral cortege returning without the bier, the torches extinguished. The lament for the dead, previously interrupted, is now resumed in front of the manorhouse with elaborate formality. In antiphonal verses the sad words of the soloists alternate with the stanzas of the mounting lament of the chorus. We learn that Admetus actually tried to leap down into the grave after the coffin was lowered but was physically prevented from doing so. His grief seems real enough now. He realizes the desolation the future holds in store for him. His bed is empty. He himself has vowed to abstain from all pleasure. His enemies will point to him contemptuously as the man who lives at the expense of his wife's life. A broken man, he stares into space. No word of comfort comes from the chorus. They sing that Alcestis will be known for her blessed deed even to the wayfarer who passes her grave.

The last, the Euripidean twist, has set in. The immortality of the heroine has been assured because of the selfishness of the hero. She died for what? For a man who is hardly a man.

The telling of the myth proceeds. The heroic Heracles has torn Alcestis out of the grip of Death. Now he returns, leading her silent form by the hand. He approaches the group sunk in misery at the threshold of the manorhouse. Admetus starts up in surprise. He had quite forgotten Heracles. He looks at the mysterious form, young and slender, who is robed in a white veil under her black garments. He does not recognize her, but a certain uneasiness fills him with apprehension.

Heracles must punish Admetus for deceiving him. He stages a play within the play, a comedy that turns the tragic drama into a mirthful satire.

Heracles puts Admetus to the test. He says he has won the woman as a prize in an athletic contest. He asks Admetus to be good enough to house this woman for him until he has finished his labors in the north, when he will return to claim her. Admetus takes the bait, but assumes his role of the bereaved, inconsolable husband. The woman cannot stay in Alcestis's home. But his eyes are irresistibly drawn to her. Like the mocking Euripides, we know, of course, that she is indeed Alcestis, but Admetus does not know that yet.

Heracles sustains his jest until the last. His sense of humor crackles like a flash of summer lightning. In mock sorrow he laments that his insufficient strength prevents him retrieving Alcestis from Hades. Heracles takes the veiled woman by the hand and leads her to the man who does not dare to look at her. Admetus pleads that he must honor his wife's memory, but Heracles skeptically dismisses his words. Men get over that kind of idealism all too easily, and all sensible men know that love is soon forgotten.

Once again the desperate widower calls to mind his pledge to his dying wife, claiming that he will choose death over betrayal of the wife who had been so true and loving. Heracles simply takes no notice of this. Thundering that Admetus is to obey him, he pushes the woman toward Admetus.

Admetus struggles with himself. Where does honor lie? Is he to hold steadfast to his duty to his dead wife. Or is he to act upon his duty of hospitality to the living, his guest? Let it be as it must be. The "hero" in him gives way, conceding that the woman can be brought into his house.

But Heracles, masterful and unrelenting, says he will give her into Admetus's hands alone.

Admetus, with face averted, grasps her outstretched hand. Their hands touch. Heracles clasps their hands together. Then turning his attention to them for a last time, he impatiently orders Admetus to look into the eyes of the woman and tell him if he is not willing to have her as a wife.

The jest has gone far enough. Heracles cannot

afford the time to play this game any longer, however enjoyable it may be. He must shoulder his famous cudgel and go on into the far distance into the night. Trembling, Admetus parts her veils.

Happy ending! The king throws off his black mourning cloak. He calls for a festival. Torches! Music! Now, he exults, they can lead a better life.

Will their lives be better? We can only hope so.

The reader should keep in mind that *Alcestis* was produced as the last unit of a tetralogy, in the position of the satyr play that usually followed the drama trilogy.

Medea

Jason, the hero of the legend of the Argonauts, has carried off the golden fleece, famed in mythology, from Colchis on the Black Sea. As reward for this feat he was to get the throne usurped by his father's half-brother, Pelias. He could never have succeeded in stealing this prize in that distant land if he had not had the help there of the king's daughter, the princess Medea. She fell madly in love with him, and with her magic potions she put the dragons who guarded the treasure to sleep. Then, by murdering her brother, she made Jason's escape possible and fled with him.

After adventurous travels, Jason brought the fleece home to Iolcus, where he expected it would help him to obtain his father's throne. In spite of his hopes, the throne was denied him. To aid him, Medea devised a stratagem. Deceived by Medea's promise that she could put Pelias together and make him young again by the use of her magic mixtures, Pelias's own daughters killed him and cut him into pieces.

Pelias's son now drove Jason and Medea with their children out of Iolcus. Becoming refugees, they found temporary asylum in Corinth, where King Creon has a daughter but no son. Jason has wooed and won the hand of Princess Glauce. According to Hellenic law, a man could enter into a marriage without a divorce from a previous wife. In Jason's case, he was especially free to act because his earlier marriage to Medea had been contracted with only barbarian oaths. He has already moved into the royal palace, while Medea and her children and some of her servants remain in the temporary refugee quarters.

Medea's old nurse comes out of the refugee lodge. She laments the brooding, gloomy despair into which her mistress has fallen. The children come back, romping with a ball, from a stroll they have been taking with their tutor. The tutor has heard the latest news, which is that Medea is to be told to leave.

Wild lamentation is now heard from within the shelter. It grows into a piercing song of Medea's resentment and denunciation. Her wailing has startled and stirred up the women of the neighborhood. In sympathy with her, they hasten to the scene. Their fellow feeling for Medea welds them into solidarity with her in her misfortune, in spite of her being an alien barbarian. The fate of women is the same everywhere.

Now Medea emerges from the lodge. A blonde woman, she is clothed in the Hellenic style. There is nothing to mark her as the wild sorceress, nothing to indicate her infamous reputation. She conceals the desperation of her state, now that she appears in public. She speaks to the women calmly and reasonably. Knowing now what threatens her, she is intelligent enough to listen quietly to King Creon, who arrives, accompanied by his bodyguard. He announces the order of deportation to her.

Medea confronts three men in the first half of the play. Each has more than one dramatic function in the action. Each stands as the representative of his sex against her as the representative of hers. Each of them speaks for his own generation. Jason is young. Creon is a white-bearded old man. Aegeus is in his forties.

Medea opposes each of them with the weapons and the consciousness of her attractive femininity. She is handsome and proud. She has magnetic charm.

By hypocritically throwing herself at Creon's knees, she succeeds in winning from him a concession of one day's delay in carrying out the order of banishment. She needs this time to carry out the program of vengeance she is planning, for she will not stand for being ridiculed by her enemies. Then Creon becomes angry at his own weakness in dealing with her. "I was not born to be a tyrant," he confesses. Finally he hurls his decree at her. She will be subjected to death by stoning if she fails to leave Corinth the very next day.

The scene demonstrates Medea's irresistible effect on men. This is due not to any of her magic arts, but only to the glamor of her womanhood. Euripides is clear about what he is doing. It is the destiny of women.

This woman, with her children, is being deserted by her husband. That was and is not unusual. It was regarded as perfectly ethical in the Hellas of that time. The wife had no opportunity to protest or to seek legal redress. Had she dared to do the same thing, she would have had to account for it.

Jason's treatment of Medea was considered acceptable by his society. The Hellenic women in the chorus realize it is futile to rebel against this treatment. Reason dictates they must reconcile themselves to male oppression. But Medea is not prepared to accept the male code so supinely. Her willfulness is due not to her barbarian inheritance but to her innate heroism. From their myths the Hellenes knew many such women who refused to reconcile themselves.

One of the women tells Medea that she is not the first woman to be so victimized. They advise her not to feel such bitterness over what cannot be changed. But she will not surrender submissively. She determines to use the power she herself possesses, that which has little to do with law and custom, and to apply her knowledge and audacity to what has happened to her. In the name of her sex, she challenges the lords of her world.

Medea's plan for vengeance has now been perfected. Jason enters. There is not much more that can be said about him. This is the man with whom Medea was deeply in love, for whose sake she did so much that was frightful and criminal. He was her ideal, to whom she devoted herself entirely. His bearing is that of an aristocrat. Every gesture he makes shows his superior breeding. He is every inch the gentleman, the pattern every young man in Hellas would wish to emulate.

Jason is not conscious of having acted shamefully to Medea. He has merely done what any man in his place would do. Through his marriage to Princess Glauce he is now prince consort and heir to the throne of Corinth. What is useful is good. This is what he tries to explain to Medea. He wanted to get out of this hovel on the outskirts of the city. He wanted to achieve a better life for himself and bring up his children as their lineage entitles them to be raised. It would eventually benefit their mother as well. That is all there is to it.

And all this would have gone smoothly if only Medea had acted sensibly. But she has gone about shrieking for justice and uttering threats against the royal family. Can one blame them if they resent such talk and wish her out of the country? Unfortunately, their animosity has spread to the children. Princess Glauce has insisted that Medea and her children be sent away. But Medea unfortunately thinks only about having Jason in bed with her. It is this way of thinking that a cultivated gentleman despises to the uttermost. He does not permit himself to be controlled by his passions. He keeps his head clear and bears himself irreproachably. It is not his way to allow his feelings free play as Medea does. Then, as now, it is easy to foresee his conclusion: Medea must understand that the necessary is not sordid.

What does Jason now want? To show her how big-hearted he is, he has hurried to offer her money and letters of introduction to her place of exile. He appears after hearing that Creon had granted her one more day in Corinth. Why not before? He admits that he loves his children. It will pain him to part with them, but Medea alone is to blame for that.

She persuades him to make a last effort to obtain permission for the children to live in the palace at Corinth. It would take only a little good will from the others to accomplish that much. Jason, believing he knows how to manipulate the royal family, agrees to arrange it. But why did he not try to do that before? Medea rejects his money and his letters. He is indignant and calls on the gods to witness that he has offered her everything that could be expected of him. So he leaves, as Medea calls after him to go to his wench.

Aegeus, king of Athens, happens to be passing by. Aristotle reproached Euripides for the weak motivation of this entrance. Aegeus is on his way back from Delphi, where he went to consult Apollo about his childlessness. He is on his way to Troezen, a city on the northwest coast of the Peloponnesus well known to Athenians. Troezen is the birthplace of Theseus, the national hero of Athens. Aegeus, the third man in this drama, will be the progenitor of Theseus, though at this point his supposed impotence has not yet been cured. Vigorous, jovial, impressive, he is in the prime of life. Medea and Jason are old acquaintances of his. He greets Medea warmly when he sees her and stops his royal train. It is a joyful meeting for him.

Medea has just been giving vent to her sorrows. She seizes the opportunity to talk. Aegeus has turned up as if she had sent for him. His appearance would also explain her later residence in Athens, according to the

tradition. He asks why she is grieving. When Medea
confides that Jason has deserted her, he responds with
indignation. To her complaint that Jason cannot be
faithful, he tells her to let him go. So far, so good.
But now she exposes Jason's perfidy. Who is her successor? The crown princess of Corinth. Taken aback,
Aegeus now understands why she is so unhappy.

But, Medea tells him, that is not the worst of it. She
has been banished from Corinth. Aegeus is stern that
Jason is permitting that. Now, however, he restrains
his indignation. There is a disconcerting silence, after
which Aegeus's switch becomes apparent. Nothing
remains of his first spontaneous reaction of shock.
Aegeus is fearful of being involved in complications.
Athens, Corinth—this could become a political issue.

Medea grasps the initiative. For the second time
she shows her magic power. For the second time she
drops to her knees before a man. She grasps his
hand, begging him to take her into his home. But it is
not as simple as all that. She knows what men are
like. She must offer something in exchange. She
promises that the gods will reward him for his gen-
erosity. But what is more to the point, she will give
him drugs that will enable him to beget children. A
long silence. Aegeus makes no effort to raise Medea
from her knees. He has to make a political decision.
Eventually, he arrives at a crafty solution.

He will guarantee Medea asylum. But he cannot
take her with him out of Corinth. She must first leave
Corinth on her own and then seek refuge in Athens.
There she may live in safety. He will hand her over
to no one.

But Medea has in mind the enormity of the deeds

she intends to perform before leaving Corinth. What would Aegeus do if he were requested by Corinth to hand her over? She rises. Seizing upon his offer, she asks him to take a vow. It is a great moment for her in the play. With impressive power she prescribes the oath he must swear. He repeats it obediently, following her dictation. She coerces him into agreeing that should he violate his vow he will submit to the punishment that is imposed on one guilty of sacrilege. With this he departs. No word of farewell.

Another man. Like all the rest. This one will be the father of democracy. He thinks only of his own advantage. She calls good wishes after him.

The second half of the play whips past, rushed along because the action, according to the rules of classical tragedy, must be completed within the span of one day. Carried along by emotional excitement, the action builds up toward the climax, which is the murder of the children. Why is this necessary? Why must the children die? Medea, obsessed by her plan of vengeance, shows a kind of cold frenzy coupled with the utmost sagacity.

In a long monologue, Medea discloses the steps of her scheme. She will ask Jason to return. Pretending to be submissive, she will ask his pardon. She will pretend to be reconciled. She will play upon his trust to make him her instrument, getting him to take gifts from her children to the palace.

One gift will be a frock of wondrous beauty, impregnated with a fiery poison. The princess will put it on. The poison will begin its work only when the children are on the way home to their mother. Then it will be mortal. The princess will feel her whole body is being eaten alive. Whoever attempts to tear the dress off her body will himself be overcome by the corroding acid. This will destroy the princess's father as well.

It is clear to Medea what will happen after the perpetration of this hideous crime. Neither she nor the children will be permitted to escape. If she wants to prevent her enemies from taking revenge on the children, she will have to kill them herself.

The scheme works out according to her plan. At first Jason refuses to take the gifts, but, when assured they are for his young bride, agrees. The children carry the small parcels with the gifts in them. Completely absorbed in carrying out her design, Medea approaches the moment that obsesses her, her moment of triumph over her enemies. In this way she arrives at the scene that will become the peak of high dramatic art for all time, her monologue before the murder of her children.

Only when things have progressed to this point does her obsession break. Her children return from the palace. Suddenly, the maternal instinct within her wells up. With the aid of the gods she has caught herself in her own net.

The death of her children was the part of her plan of vengeance that was meant to pierce Jason to the heart. Now she feels her own heart fatally pierced. Conflict begins to tear her apart. How can she take life away from the children who look at her with trusting eyes? Yet, how can she let her jeering enemies injure her without reprisal? She draws her children close to her and embraces them. Knowing what she is going to do, she cannot look at them any longer if she is to maintain her revengeful anger. The children are led into the house. At first Medea feels that she cannot do this foul deed.

But her moments of vacillation grow shorter and shorter. At last she suppresses her tender feelings. Her children are not to live their lives as targets of ridicule. Now she speaks lines that have lived through the years: the daemonic instinct that is the source of all mental ills, the need that must be satisfied above emotions, directs her clearly.

A long silent scene follows. Medea crouches on the steps like a statue. The chorus sings a deeply pensive passage. During the silence, the actor (as women's parts were always played by men) must convey by gesture the firming of her final decision. Euripides, as his own stage director, allowed Medea a long interval to communicate this to the audience.

When Medea speaks once more, she mounts a raised platform. From this she will be the first to see the messenger coming with the news of the outcome of her action. She stands there for a period, staring into the distance. She is waiting to hear some outcry, some demonstration, some message for her, some tidings. Whatever the news will be, she will have time to dash into the house, make the door fast inside, and perform the last act of her dreadful plot.

Euripides prescribed the composition of a highly expressive musical accompaniment to heighten and intensify the moments of the actual murder scene. Desperate cries are heard from within. The women outside beat a drum-fire pounding against the locked entrance door and shout imprecations against the murderer. Finally, Jason appears, utterly distraught, in

violent haste to save the children from royal vengeance, with his sword in hand to cut their mother
down. This, then, is the ending.

The conclusion is in the form of a miracle. Above
the roof of the house a flying chariot swung ex
machina in the same gondola device generally used to
produce the deus ex machina. The wings are those of
the dragons who seem to be moving it.

At its first production this glittering stage effect
must have been a most impressive success, because it
was copied innumerable times. The audience saw the
bodies of the dead children hanging through the
lattice work of the cart. Medea wears a magnificent
oriental robe, a diadem sparkles in her blonde hair.
Everything glows in the rays of the sun. Jason is left
groaning as he recoils from the door he has broken
open. From on high, Medea declaims her triumphant
verses. Her enemies can ridicule her no longer. She
will bury her children up on the promontory, the
Acrocorinth, where Hera has her temple. Then she
will fly to sanctuary in Athens.

Medea returns into the mythical aura out of which
Euripides has brought her. Here you see her, he
seems to call out to his audience, just as you would
have her be. Isn't that how you visualized her when
you came to the theater—a fury, a sorceress, a super-
woman, half-witch, half-demon.

Would she have committed such a horrifying murder had not the selfishness, the vanity, the opportunis-
tic brutality of a man forced her into an unendurable
situation, and if she could have comforted herself
with the recognition that she was not the first to submit to this lot of women?

She was not the first. It is the destiny of women.

Would it not make sense to the men, most of whom think like Jason, or to the women, who think as all women think, to bring this woman before them, who refused to submit to injustice at the hands of a man she had loved?

Medea flies off in her dragon chariot to live on as a fury. She lived on earth a short while as a human, as a woman. This was only make-believe, says Euripides. It was only a play.

Hippolytus

Theseus, the national hero of Athens and the mythical founder of democracy, has a summer residence in Troezen, on the northwest coast of the Peloponnesus, where he was born. Often staying there for prolonged periods, he has been living there for a year when the play opens. His illegitimate son Hippolytus lives there permanently with his grandfather. Hippolytus was born of a liaison with Hippolyte, queen of the Amazons, who died giving him birth.

When the play opens Theseus is away on a trip. His queen, Phaedra, daughter of the king of Crete and sister of Ariadne, is living at the royal palace with her court. She is the mother of two small legitimate sons, Acamas and Demophon, who are mentioned as kings of Athens in Euripides's *Children of Heracles*.

Aphrodite speaks the prologue. Artemis appears in the epilogue. The two goddesses are at odds with each other. Their strife is the theme of the play, love against chastity.

The first act opens in front of a castle, at the edge of the sea, surrounded by lofty mountains, steep ravines, and deep woods.

The goddess Aphrodite has barely vanished when a burst of hunting music resounds. With it appear Hippolytus, the handsome young prince, and his party of comrades, storming in from the hunt, with their spears and their game, exuding sparkling youth, gay companionship, and the carefree joy of life. The fast-moving scene is in allegro, with hunting calls, bright, cool, and refreshing as a spring of clear water. In the prologue Aphrodite had taxed Hippolytus with being a chaste transgressor who has defied her and must submit to punishment by her.

Hippolytus reveals that he ignores her because he does not worship gods who work only in the dark. So he joyfully crowns the statue of Artemis with a flowering garland. She is the goddess of the hunt and also of chastity. For the statue of Aphrodite, he has only a passing glance. Nevertheless, he is no lone wolf. Neither is he disdainful of her. It is true he shuns the formal life of the court. Sports and the hunt are the joys of him and of his companions. He differs from his group in one outstanding respect, that of his innocence and piety. More or less consciously, he has spiritualized his adolescent virginity into the glamor of divine love. He is the embodiment of male innocence as we know it in many statues of ancient art, as the counterpart of the innocent maiden.

The joyful hubbub settles down as the group disappears into the manorhouse.

A different style of music resounds. Muffled, heavy rhythms. We hear the dragging measures of the

chorus of old women in black. They come up from
the rocks by the seashore, on which they have left
the royal purple cloths to dry in the sun. They are
simple women of the neighborhood, full of concern
and curiosity. A woman who works in the castle has
disclosed to them that Phaedra is severely ill. She says
that toward evening Phaedra will have herself
brought out of the house so they will be able to see
her baffling condition for themselves.

Phaedra has taken no food for days. She hides her
face and talks about dying. We hear the clatter of the
door opening from the women's quarters of the castle. The chorus hovers around one corner of the
orchestra space. The music changes to suit the mood
of the scene.

Phaedra, heavily veiled, totters out on the arm of
her old nurse. Servants place her couch in the sun.
When Phaedra throws back her veils, the women of
the chorus take fright at the waxen whiteness of her
face. She lets her glance stray eagerly over the stage
toward the men's quarters into which Hippolytus has
disappeared, and toward the open clearing from
which he had emerged. Then she turns away, veiling
her face again. She wishes to be taken back into her
quarters. The nurse, fussy and garrulous, expresses
her irritation of Phaedra's constantly shifting moods
and whims.

Phaedra sinks down listlessly on her couch. But there
is no rest for her at all. She twists about restlessly.
Now she begins to ramble feverishly about wishing to
lie down in the meadow. We know what she is after.
She is thinking of the meadow where the young men
go for exercise.

Her mania grows. She grasps the arms of her servants to lift herself higher and talks about going into the mountains and joining the hunt.

The nurse, perplexed and frightened, assails her with questions. Phaedra sees herself with a spear in her hand. She wants to gallop on the sands by the ocean. The nurse believes Phaedra is losing her mind.

But that is only the first phase. The music dies down as the next phase begins. This one, the awakening from her spell, the return of consciousness, the terror of reality, is much worse. Phaedra turns away to hide her tears and her blush of shame. Then she sinks down in a swoon.

Now we know how to put all these symptoms together. Aphrodite gave us the clue in the prologue. Ever since the first time Phaedra saw Hippolytus in Athens, when he went there to attend a festival, she had been in love with him.

Phaedra's misfortune is that Theseus had decided to spend so long a sojourn in their summer residence. Propinquity to the object of her secret love feeds her passion daily.

The sickness of love, the effect of the arrow of Aphrodite that was meant to pierce Hippolytus the transgressor, has mounted in her until it has become a frenzy, because Hippolytus takes no notice of her at all. Keeping entirely aloof from her, he mingles only with the comrades of his own choice.

She has herself carried out of the house on some pretext, so that she can at least look at Hippolytus. The nearer the day of Theseus's return draws, the much more critical becomes the infatuated woman's condition.

Her women, having no inkling of the true cause of her illness, are filled with deep concern for her. The

nurse discloses that Phaedra wishes to die, but instead
of killing herself decisively, she has chosen the less
conclusive way of starving herself to death so as not
to prematurely deprive herself of the sight of her
beloved.

While she lies in a faint on her couch, the women
of the chorus are whispering agitatedly with her
nurse. There must be some secret they can extract
from her. If they can find the source of her illness,
they can find a doctor who can cure it. But the
nurse says that despite all her efforts she can get nothing out of Phaedra.

The nurse waddles around. Phaedra, however, is
only pretending to be in a swoon and hears everything being said about her. The nurse masterfully
practices rhetorical persuasion. She keeps casting her
hook in ever new directions. Then she says that
Phaedra should take thought of her children. Otherwise they will be ruled by Hippolytus.

Suddenly and unwittingly, she has stumbled on the
right approach. That name produces the explosion.
The mere pronouncing of his name shatters the darkness into which the unhappy queen had withdrawn in
her loneliness. She utters a stifled cry. She is torn by
an irresistible force. She forbids the nurse ever to
mention the name of Hippolytus to her again.

The truth comes out into the open suddenly. Lamentation fills the stage. The nurse is plunged into the
deepest gloom. Her actions and conduct make a
witch's caldron of the arena. First she threatens to
throw herself into the sea, but the women stand in
her way, while she tears her hair and wails unutterable
imprecations.

The chorus wails in accord with her. They throw

themselves to the ground. The floor is covered with their bodies in collapse. Then the music ceases. Silence.

Phaedra rises quietly from her couch. The great speech that follows is the high point of this half of the play. She illustrates the hopeless tragedy of one unwilling to allow herself to be a plaything of destiny. She is aware of her fate (the passion inflicted on her by the gods), which she cannot resist. Yet she is not deprived of the ability to recognize the consequences of this passion. She has brooded over this through long nights. In her plight she still has the liberty of freely chosen death.

But if she chooses death, what then? What will her husband think? What will her children and other people think of her? She has not been able to think this problem through, as suicide itself would amount to a confession of her guilt.

Now that Phaedra is hinting at death, the nurse comes to her senses. With irresistible persuasiveness she puts her shoulder to the wheel. Why die? It would be simpler and more sensible to transgress on the marriage tie if it could be arranged in secret so that no one would be the wiser. What of it? All women do it. Theseus is away. Once you have assuaged your feverish craving, we can consider what to do next.

But this is radically against Phaedra's nature. She cannot bear to act a living lie. The nurse is persuasive. She argues that Phaedra must indulge her desire to save her life.

Phaedra's reason warns her to fear the worst, but she no longer has the strength to hinder the nurse's plan of winning Hippolytus by her magic potions. She does not give her actual consent, but the nurse is already running to the men's quarters to set her plot in motion. The chorus comments that love though sweet is frightening.

But the nurse's effort is totally wrecked on the rock of Hippolytus's virtue. Phaedra is compelled to watch as he drives the would-be matchmaker away from his presence and shouts his indignation at her publicly and aloud. He knows Phaedra hears what he says. He curses the nurse because she was clever enough to bind him to secrecy about Phaedra's passion. He includes all women in his curses.

Phaedra sees him rushing away from the scene. She realizes her secret cannot be hidden much longer. She cannot go on living in constant fear that Hippolytus may reveal it. And so she cannot face Theseus on his return.

Now that she has seen Hippolytus trample her love for him underfoot, she must trample on it just as brutally herself. She will protect her good name before her husband, her children, and all the world, though the cost is the destruction of an innocent victim. She carries out the will of Aphrodite.

Theseus returns. He was not expected so soon. When he pushes his door open, he finds Phaedra's body hanging inside. They carry it out. While the pathos of lamentation fills the stage, Theseus notices a writing tablet fastened to her arm. Reading it, the scales fall from his eyes. He is enraged. Hippolytus arrives with his comrades. Theseus flings at him the accusation that he has dishonored his father's bed.

This then was Phaedra's last weapon. She wrote that she had to kill herself because Hippolytus had violated her. He was sworn to secrecy by his oath to the nurse. Theseus curses him and banishes him. The scene in which the two men confront each other has tragic greatness. Theseus orders his bodyguard to seize his son and evict him.

Hippolytus orders the men to stay away from him. If he is to be thrust out of his country it must be by his father's hand. Theseus answers that if Hippolytus doesn't go immediately he will do just that.

Theseus follows the bier into the palace. Hippolytus, left alone in despair, turns to the statue of Artemis and complains that he cannot reveal the truth about Phaedra. He says good-bye to Athens and to Troezen. Then, taking leave of his comrades, he maintains his innocence no matter what his father believes.

After a most agitated musical interlude comes an overwhelming report brought by a messenger. The working of the curse of Aphrodite becomes apparent in the graphic description the messenger brings of a fatal accident to Hippolytus. In his chariot, in which he was leaving the kingdom, he was hit by an earthquake and tidal wave. His horses were catapulted into the sea. He suffered fearful wounds. His broken body is being brought onto the stage, on a bier by his comrades. He wears a mangled mask.

A hymn of lamentation glorifies Aphrodite's fearful power. While the procession bearing the dying youth is still in motion, the goddess Artemis appears above the palace in the machina. The bier is set down. Theseus perseveres in his hot anger. The gods have destroyed whom they have condemned. The song of the dying youth grips the hearts of all. At the moment that Hippolytus feels Artemis close to him, his pain is soothed by the holiness that becomes tangible to him.

Artemis narrates the truth of the whole sad episode. When she vanishes, the stage is suffused with the feeling of humanity, forgiveness, reconciliation, and understanding. Thus the art of theater proves the reality of the invisible powers. They are glorious and cruel: they are gods. When they are in conflict with each other, their victims perish. Phaedra and Hippolytus die because Aphrodite insists on exerting her power. But Artemis declares that the next sacrifice will demonstrate hers. It will be Adonis, the protegé of Aphrodite, whom Artemis will lay low.

The play won a first prize in Athens. No drama is more widely read, renowned, and imitated. Why, in view of this, was it superseded on the stages of Europe by Racine's *Phèdre*, which Schiller translated into German? Certainly not for the reason offered by Racine as an explanation as to why he altered the plot so radically. Racine let Phaedra die without leaving the letter behind and made the nurse guilty of casting suspicion on Hippolytus. He said: "I thought the calumny was entirely too despicable and devious to be attributed to a princess who otherwise cherished such noble and virtuous sentiments."

Nowadays we no longer demand that our protagonists be so flawless. The device of the letter is really the crux of the story. A convention used for the first time on the stage, it has become through the centuries a necessary ingredient of the stage. The way Phaedra makes this letter known to all strikes one as wanton and also embarrassing. Hippolytus is only a fictional creation. But Phaedra lives.

Ion

Creusa, daughter of Erechtheus, the mythical ancestor of the kings of Athens (to whom the Erechtheum, the sacred edifice on the Acropolis, is dedicated), is the last of her line. She was impregnated by the god Apollo in a cavern under the Acropolis. She gave birth to her child secretly in the same cavern, for who would have believed that it had been fathered by Apollo?

She had set the infant out there in a little basket, swathed in a prettily decorated wrapping, confident that Apollo would come and rescue his own son. Next day, in fear wild beasts might have harmed it, she went to look for it. Her basket with the child in it had vanished.

Years later she consented to a political marriage to Xuthus, king of the island of Euboea, who knew nothing of this episode in her past. He had rendered Athens decisive aid in a perilous war. The marriage is childless, but now the people of Athens are demanding an heir. The royal couple have resolved to make a pilgrimage to Delphi to consult the oracle.

Hermes, messenger of the gods, betrays the secret to us in a prologue. He himself, at Apollo's bidding, had taken good care of Creusa's infant, and had set it down on the threshold of Apollo's temple at Delphi. There, the Pythia, who prophesies over the tripod, had found the child and brought it up. The boy, now sixteen, has received the best of upbringing. He is living in the temple, working as the caretaker of the temple treasures.

But now, as Hermes tells us, the day has come for Apollo to grant his son the honor for which he was destined, of being named king of Athens.

The stage setting presents a rural idyll. At the front of the stage, the façade of the temple of Apollo can be seen. In the dim light of the rising sun, Hermes, the god of the prologue, has emerged out of the shadows of the darkening laurel bushes around the portico, and has vanished into them again. We hear music, the silvery voices of three boys running on stage, one of whom is Ion. He sends his companions down to the Castalian spring to fetch water while he himself begins the routine tasks of his temple service. He grasps a bough of laurel with which to sweep the steps. From a jug he sprinkles water on the marble.

First he greets the sun, which has risen above Parnassus and floods his handsome half-profile with its rays. He sings praises to Apollo while he goes about his duties. The combination of realistic prosaic elements with others that are highly poetic, even holy, produces an effect as of enchantment. The appearance of the young curator as the embodiment of purity, moving before a soaring musical accompaniment, combined with his movements as he performs his homey chores, creates for us the essence of all we recall about the mystery of delphic utterance.

The sacred has never been portrayed with less solemnity, with such matter-of-course realism. As Ion grasps his bow to scare off birds that threaten to swoop down onto the sacrificial offerings, the music of his song of praise quickens in a stretto. He chases the birds away with the twang of his bow but has not the heart to shoot them down with his arrows.

When he turns again to his work, the chorus approaches with music. We soon learn they are young Athenian maidens, eager, excited, swift-footed, who have accompanied their queen, Creusa, to Delphi. It is their first opportunity to visit the famed temple at Delphi. They had arrived the evening before. Xuthus, their king, is not with them because he stopped to consult another oracle along the way. This was most welcome to Creusa, who had her own secret business to discuss with Apollo. She has come now to face the father of her child and demand a reckoning from him.

This is not known to the maidens. The solo of the youth is followed by the chorus of the maidens, revealing their charming curiosity. They rush here and there like typical tourists, exclaiming over the sculptured figures on the pediments and the metopes of the temple structure. They are fascinated.

Ion seems almost to be forgotten by them. Silently, and with perhaps exaggerated self-importance, he goes on with his duties. The maidens pretend they are taking no notice of him, but presently a few of them dance prettily up to the zealous caretaker with a question. Their leader asks if they may go inside. As if they do not know! Then the chorus asks him what is inside the temple. As if they do not know what every child in Hellas is taught!

Ion pauses to supply information with didactic strictness.

Here comes Creusa with her retinue. They bring the ritual gift offerings. Ion's glance falls on the eminent visitor in gorgeous raiment, wearing her crown, who now walks toward the temple. A silent scene, such as only a great dramatist can create.

We know they are mother and son, for Hermes has told us so. Creusa is constrained to act the reserved, inscrutable queen. But she is consumed with her dammed-up hatred for Apollo, which later in the play she will shriek out in blasphemous fury.

Creusa catches sight of Ion. He is exactly the same age as her own child should be. He is, in fact, her very own. How is it that the inexplicable call of nature does not overpower her at once? She breaks into tears. Ion is moved as if by a stroke of lightning. As yet we know little about him, but we start to know him better as he talks to Creusa. He is more than just a handsome saint. Apollo has also endowed him with thirst for knowledge and reflectiveness.

When he began to be aware of himself, he also began to ask questions to which he got no answer. "Who is my father? Who is my mother?" He has brooded over the mystery of his birth. He is lonely, though surrounded by divinity whom he loves and to whom he is utterly devoted. More than anything he yearns for the mother love he has never had.

The high cultivation that has been bred into him by those who raised him has sharpened his intelligence. His desire for knowledge is something like the need that drove Oedipus. He often asks piercing questions like an inquisitor.

Creusa will say to him that she is "seemingly happy but unhappy." That is Ion's plight as well. He is torn by the contrast between the peaceful harmony of his surroundings and his consuming thirst to know. Now for the first time he stands before a woman whom he does not feel indifference toward, and he sees this woman in tears. Deep alarm makes him cry out. Sympathy for her and dismay at his feelings have broken his handsome presence. At the end, he will himself confess that at their first meeting he could have believed Creusa was his mother.

The dialogue that follows is marked by an irony that gives it double meaning. It borders on the uncanny. It is the longest dialogue exchange in all the tragedies of Euripides. The childless mother, the motherless youth; they are both so awash in sympathy for each other that they forget the presence of the chorus.

Ion's "Who are you?" dominates the first half of their colloquy. The second opens with Creusa's "But who are you?" The music heard during the introductory idyll stops at this point. In the long dialogue that follows, the truth is half revealed by Creusa and Ion, and then withdrawn and concealed for fear it will be disclosed.

Creusa claims she has come to inquire on behalf of a friend. She tells her story as one that happened to another. She tells Ion that the child would be his age now. He remarks how alike his fate is to the child Creusa is telling him about.

Then the tempo begins to accelerate. The tension in the dialogue grows as Ion warns Creusa not to try Apollo's patience by pressing him for a reply. He will refuse to disclose what he wishes to conceal. Creusa must agree it must be so. She has more at stake than only her private destiny. This is well understood by the Athenian audience. If she cannot find her own child the line of Erechtheus will be extinguished, as will the race from which Theseus is to spring. She is the last survivor of her family.

The conflict is vital at this political juncture, because Creusa's husband is an alien. If he gets a son who is not hers, the polis of Athens will fall into foreign hands. This brings Creusa's personal destiny out into a fateful connection with Athen's destiny. As we in the audience know who Ion really is, we know also that he is to be torn from his life of peace and beauty. He must depart from his idyllic privacy in order to step out into the full glare of the great world outside.

The dialogue ends in action. Ion forbids Creusa access to the sanctuary. She has no right to press Apollo for an answer. Swooning with indignation, Creusa retreats. Facing the temple, she cries out accusingly to Apollo that he has abandoned his own son. The startled youth hears this blasphemy. At this moment, sounds approaching from the right, announce that the king has arrived.

Creusa silences herself. She must speak to Ion again at once. She tells him that she might be suspect, meddling in these secret affairs, if Ion should disclose what has driven her there. Ion makes no reply and leaves her. She feels apprehensive. With a supreme effort she gathers herself together, but the king notices her confusion.

Creusa asks about the oracle Xuthus had stopped to consult. It could not yield anything because it did not wish to prejudge the answer of the god of Delphi. Xuthus makes his arrangements. He will enter the temple alone. Ion lets the door be opened for the royal entry. Creusa must wait outside alone. She can only pray for a favorable outcome.

When the door into the sanctuary is shut behind the king, Creusa has reached the lowest depth of her humiliation: she must accept whatever the god gives her because he is a god. She goes off.

Ion remains alone. He reaches for a jug to go on with his duties, but he broods over the fate of the woman of whom he has learned. He sees himself confronted by a situation in which the god he reveres has not conducted himself nobly. He is perturbed. Is it fair to call men evil when the gods themselves perpetrate evil?

He disappears into the temple arcade. The Athenian girls implore the gods. They ask a blessing, not for Xuthus but for Creusa, for her lineage threatened with extinction.

Ion returns. Now he carries the insignia of his religious duties, the wreath in his hair, the bow in his hand. The verse meter accelerates. There is an air of agitated expectation. The temple door is opened. Xuthus hurries out. He sees Ion and rushes over to embrace him. The oracle foretold, he says, that the first person he sees on leaving the temple is his son.

As usual, Apollo has expressed himself in ambiguities. Ion, who does not know this, is annoyed. Impatiently he waves the importunate king aside, averting his embrace. The scene borders on the embarrassing. Ion is persuaded only with difficulty. He is inclined to cross-examine Xuthus. Xuthus must know if it is possible that he be his son. Xuthus admits that about the time Ion was begotten he had made love to a maiden at the Delphic revels. At last Ion accepts this new situation. But he cannot quell the anxious fear that he will never see his mother's face.

Xuthus complies with the political consequences. Ion must return with him at once to Athens and be installed as successor to the throne. Ion is reluctant to do this.

Euripides now assigns to Ion the speech that hints at the basic meaning of the play. Ion's quiet, religious life in beautiful surroundings must give way to the reality of public life. Ion has enough intelligence and imagination to think things through more thoroughly than his "father." What will the Athenians say if the son of an alien, one who is possibly the bastard son of a slave girl, were to mount the throne of their famed city? At Delphi he has been witness to plenty of politics and learned to know politicians from all over the world. He understands how potent public opinion is. He knows the power of defamation. And then there is the barren queen, descended from an ancient line, who is supposed to accept the child of a stranger. How many people, Ion reminds Xuthus, have been killed for such reasons.

Xuthus recognizes the validity of this point. He then suggests a cheap stratagem: Ion is first to be a guest in the royal palace, and they will get Creusa to accept him so that she will give her consent to his being made the crown prince.

As against this, Ion sets the happy life he has led so far in Delphi. What are power and wealth, the commotion and glamor of the outside world, compared to this? He asks Xuthus to let him stay where he is happy, though he realizes well he cannot evade his destiny. Ion obeys Xuthus's wish, though struggling against it, that they have a majestic birthday celebration.

What will become of Creusa? The maidens cry the injustice of it to heaven, claiming that a fraud is being committed here. They insist that, whatever may be done to them, they will not remain silent. Ion and Xuthus are already celebrating. Ion must die.

Now Creusa comes in. A very old man, her former teacher who was also her father's teacher, leans on her arm for support. It becomes clear why she has brought him. She needs a witness to the claim she will make. A mysterious air of secrecy pervades the scene. The maidens are aghast but they whisper the news of what has happened. Creusa wails aloud at the first intimation of it. This youth! Her god cannot possibly do this to her too!

The music is augmented by the unearthly singing of the verses, as Creusa's pain is expressed in beauty. She collapses completely among the pillars, wishing that she could fly into the stars.

The old man sees his suspicions confirmed. It has all gone "according to plan." The oracle was manipulated. Xuthus must have known for a long time that a child he begot outside of marriage was serving in Apollo's temple at Delphi. "Xuthus it is, not the god Apollo, who deceives us with lies"—it is the powerful voice of mythical law echoing out of the old man.

The voice of the mythical law has to be protected from any alien usurpers. Even beyond that, the instinct of self-defense prevails. If the two of them intend to seize Creusa's throne, they will have every reason to do away with the true heiress.

All eyes turn to Creusa. The music sounds out again. Pathos infuses her great solo. She sings her secret to the audience. All the world shall know, now in front of Apollo's temple, how he has deceived one human, who now stands up to raise her complaint of bitterness and hate. He has granted the joy of fatherhood to Xuthus, but he has left their own child to be devoured by birds of prey. What a perfidious bedmate the great god Apollo is.

An antipaean of like horror had probably never been spoken in any Hellenic tragedy. It is the midpoint and the highpoint of the play. We in the audience know of course that her accusation is false, but it is exactly this consideration that intensifies the tragedy that Euripides now stages. For Apollo would let it happen that mother and son will come within a hair's breadth of killing each other. Can one see the hand of a god in this hair's-breadth risk?

What is to be done? Again Creusa rejects all the proposals the old man puts forward in a lengthy dialogue with her, until his talk comes to Ion. Freud would have called her reaction overcompensation. The "voice of nature" stirs up its opposite in her. Yes, a fabled poison is available to her to use. The old man takes it with him. He will mingle with the guests in the festival tent and, at a moment when he is unobserved, he will drop the poison into Ion's wine cup. Creusa's verses are cold: This drink is for the one who means to rule over my house. He will never reach

glorious Athens. In Delphi he will remain and die.
She rushes away. The chorus echoes Creusa's hatred: how dare that bastard reach for the crown of Athens. How shameful for Athens to be ruled by such as he. The chorus, as often in Euripides, serves to occupy the passage of an interval of time. For here comes one of Creusa's slaves running to find her. She is being sought after, and officers have been sent to arrest her. The man is to warn her that her life is in danger. Her women are threatened with the same punishment. The council of Delphi has pronounced the decree: death by stoning. And it was Ion who demanded it.

Flying haste! In spite of it the messenger reports in great detail the arrangements for the feast. The polis of Athens was invited to send a representative to Delphi. The whole population of Delphi was invited. A gigantic tent was pitched. It was there that the murder attempt took place. Ion lifted his cup into which the old man had poured the poison to drink, but he emptied the wine from it on the ground, irate because someone near him had uttered an obscene imprecation. So again his purity protected him. But one of the doves flying about in the tent sipped the poisoned wine on the ground and perished.

We know Ion. He quickly extracted a confession from the old man. Then he cried out: Poison from the daughter of Erechtheus has been brought to his sacred country. There we have the confrontation again: Delphi against Athens; the sacred against the worldly. The messenger closes with the warning that Creusa is being hunted down like a criminal by the whole city.

Deathly fear drives the Athenian maidens across the

stage. But where to go? Creusa rushes in, flying from her pursuers. She has only just barely eluded them. Where to? Which way? Only one place of refuge remains. It is Apollo's altar. On the altar of the gods the right of sanctuary for those pursued is sacred. The blood of the murdered would stain the altar. Euripides has brought his plot to the point where Apollo must protect one who hates him but who comes to him for protection.

The pursuing soldiers, fully armed, headed by Ion brandishing his naked sword, are storming onto the stage. He hurls frightful curses at Creusa, but hesitates when he detects her clinging to the altar. There follows a spirited, profoundly dialectical dialogue, culminating in Creusa's countercharge that Ion has tried to usurp what belongs to the house of Erechtheus.

Ion defends himself: he took only what his father gave him. He accuses Creusa of talking falsely about lineage and the polis—she has tried to kill him because her barrenness has made her bitter and envious. He repeats, when Creusa charges him with trying to snatch the property of the childless, that he has the right to inherit what is his father's. But Creusa reminds him that all Xuthus has true rights to are his shield and his sword.

We know Ion's thoughts. He himself now realizes she has bested him in this verbal exchange.

Since Creusa refuses to leave the altar, Ion gives the order to tear her away from it by force. But Creusa rises to her full height and dares him to kill her in the shrine. How could Apollo's servant take it on himself to violate Apollo's temple? He holds back.

Now the stage grouping is set dramatically. Creusa is at the altar near the central entrance. The chorus, bowed down with fear, is in the orchestra. On the right of Creusa are the armed soldiers, in front of them on the steps, Ion with his drawn sword in his hand.

The main door clanks open. It is a solemn moment. The priestess herself steps into the light, carrying a small basket in her arms. Now we realize the solution cannot be long postponed. The prophetess knows, of course, that the time has come for her to appear and conclude what she has set in motion. The day has come when she must surrender to the foundling those things that may help him to find his own mother.

When Ion cries out that he will search for his mother all through Europe and Asia, the Pythia smiles back at him ambiguously. She suggests that he start his search here in Delphi.

Over all the years, why had she never before handed over to him the little basket, with its ornaments and rich wrappings, that Creusa would have recognized? Ion had begged so often for some knowledge of his mother. There is no other answer but that only now can the story be told.

Emotion fills the stage. Ion, who has lowered his sword, hesitantly opens the little basket after the Pythia has again withdrawn into the innermost holiness of the temple. The steps in the mutual recognition of mother and son, a scene traditional in the tragedies, are beautifully fitted together. There is solemn music. The near-murderer and the near-murderess embrace each other, murmuring endearments. Exultingly, Creusa says that the heir has been found. "The home has its hearth, the land its rulers. Erechtheus has risen anew!" Trembling, mother and son recall what has just been happening. Creusa says that she was pushed by powerful fate. And she adds, "Fate flings us hither and yon, now into sorrow and again into joy. And the winds of fate change their courses at will."

Euripides has one more last irony in his design. It is almost gay. Ion does not know whether he can believe his mother that Apollo is his father. Only a goddess can answer that question. And so Athena appears in the gondola over the roof; she will complete the actions of the higher powers as the dea ex machina. She affirms it was really Apollo who made love to the maiden Creusa. A mythical luster illumines the chosen woman and the child of the god. Now Ion says good-bye to Apollo.

This incomparable play still awaits realization on our stage. T. S. Eliot, however, used the outline of *Ion* for his *Confidential Clerk*.

The Trojan Women

Troy, fallen after ten years of war, has gone up in flames. The victors have acted like enraged beasts. Even the gods who fought on their side are repelled by their conduct. Virgin priestesses have been violated at their altars.

The Trojan women have been herded into the Hellenic encampment. In the tents they wait to learn their fate. Hecuba bemoans the loss of her slain husband, Priam, king of Troy, and of her sons, not one of whom is left alive. Her daughter Polyxena and her daughter-in-law Andromache have already been dragged into captivity. Her daughter Cassandra, the priestess, the seer, the profaned one, is left with her, as is Helen, the infamous, the cause of everything that has happened. The Hellenes have not yet decided how to dispose of her.

The gods know better. In the prologue, Poseidon emerges from the sea and Athena materializes from on high. In the war, he fought on the side of the

Trojans, she for the Hellenes. Now they will join forces to punish the shameful victors. The sentence of the gods has been pronounced before the drama begins. Most of those who are gloating now over their triumph will soon be uttering lamentations. Some will get to their homes in Hellas only after indescribable suffering, and others will be overtaken by their punishment when they arrive.

This is the background that determines all that is happening. All is to appear under the shadow of what the future will make it to be. Nothing is what it appears to be.

Even during the prologue, one notices Cassandra's dark form, as she huddles at the entrance to the central tent, with her black cloak drawn up over her head. She stirs. She raises her head and sits up. Her shorn hair is now white, her face is sallow. Lamenting music is heard. Hecuba is keening, in the monotone of mourners, that they must mourn for burning Ilium.

Hecuba calls the Trojan women out of their tents. They emerge, women and girls, with their locks shorn. They step into ritual dance prescribed for burials, trembling violently with fear. Noise has startled the elders. They expect the decisions on their future fates. The Hellenes are making ready to depart. The war booty is being loaded onto the ships. The women know they are part of the spoils. Only a shred of hope runs through their laments such as mention of the rumor that there is much that is beautiful in the lands and cities to which they are to be carried off.

A signal crashes through the air. Talthybius, the

officer in charge, arrives at the head of a detachment of troops. He speaks his message while the
women continue their keening.

He is willing to answer questions. He is the type
of S.S. killer who grows sentimental at home under
the Christmas tree. Now he becomes self-important
and pretends to be gracious. First of all: they will
not stay together; therefore they should ask questions singly.

What, Hecuba asks, is to be done with Cassandra?
The old woman continues to hope that what has already happened to Cassandra is the worst. Cassandra
has been violated. But a more terrible fate is in store
for her. It is that Agamemnon, commander-in-chief of
the enemy forces, has chosen her to share his bed.
She is to accompany him to Argos as his personal concubine. This will give malicious joy to his wife, Clytemnestra, Helen's sister.

Still, Hecuba does not inquire about her own fate.
What about Polyxena and Andromache, who were
separated from the other Trojan women earlier? The
officer gives an ambiguous reply about Polyxena. We
learned in the prologue, however, that she was slain
on the grave of Achilles as a sacrifice for a favoring
wind, as Iphigenia was sacrificed before her. Andromache has been promised to Achilles's son. Hecuba
accepts this news without a word. Now at last she
asks what will become of herself.

Again she hears the saddest possible verdict. Odysseus wants her for his personal slave. This reduces her
to the uttermost despair. She beats her breast and
tears at her cheeks. Shrill shrieks from the flutes
heighten the effect of her terror.

"To be a slave to that enemy of truth, that infamous man who is indifferent to law! Weep for me, women of Troy!" she laments. She behaves as though she had suffered a stroke. Gasping for breath, she breaks down completely. The women press close around the officer. He chases them away. His order to the men is that they are to take Cassandra, then the others.

The soldiers have hardly begun to strike their tents when they fall back. Torchlight lights up the stage. What can this be? Have the women set fire to the tents? But Hecuba says that it is her child Cassandra, raging in a frenzied passion. The tent is torn open. Cassandra, brandishing a flaming torch, plunges out in an ecstatic dance. But her mind is clear. Her mother must join her in her dance. Through her prophetic vision she sees the journey home of the victors. Defiant is the marriage chant she intones for herself, for the man whose bed she is delegated to share will not live long enough to enjoy his prize. She gives way to the wild laughter that makes Talthybius snort. He would not have this mad woman in his bed for anything. Yet she is the choice of the mighty Agamemnon.

She foresees that Hecuba will never reach Ithaca. If only Odysseus knew this! Cassandra's destiny, through a curse of the gods, is that no one on the stage believes her. But the spectators know what will befall the Hellenic victors. She tears the priestess's ornaments from her head and flings them into the air at Apollo.

Hecuba has collapsed. The women drag her to the steps of her tent. There she huddles inanimately, while the women chant the burial song for Ilium.

Andromache crouches on a four-wheeled cart that

comes rumbling in drawn by slaves. The wagon is piled full of war booty. She is perched atop it, with Hector's little son in her arms. She is able to tell Hecuba what happened to Polyxena, who was perhaps the luckiest of all: "Being dead is the same as not being born." Better to die than live in misery. The dead feel no evil, feel no pain.

Andromache speaks of her happiness with Hector, living quietly at home, being loyal, gentle, content. Thus Helen's image is shown in contrast. Exactly what made for Andromache's good name is what is to cause her ruin, for it is for these virtues that Achilles's son has chosen her as his wife. It is said that one night of love dissolves a woman's aversion to a man. Not so for Andromache. She is worse than dead because she has lost hope. She will never know happiness again.

As Andromache descends from the cart, Hecuba tries to comfort her. Many women have learned to be happy with a second husband. Hector's child needs a father; Andromache can serve her husband's people if she raises her child to become Troy's future savior.

Euripides puts into Hecuba's mouth the words that have been weighed and argued in the Hellenic quarters. Now Talthybius returns with his military escort. He tears the child out of its mother's arms. Troy must not have a future savior. Reasons of state demand the death of the child. Andromache tries to cling to him. Talthybius has his big scene now. Andromache, who has lost her husband and her land, must submit to the victor's power. Her child is to be hurled to death from the walls of Troy. Why struggle when she is powerless? If she accepts her grief bravely, she can at least hope that her child will get a decent burial.

Andromache's farewell to her little one has become famous. Her tender last words to him pull at one's heartstrings. When the child is finally taken from her, this quiet gentle soul becomes a raging lioness. She flings curses into the face of the Hellenes: They are barbarians; let them kill the child; let them eat him like the savages they are. She is forced back into the cart. The slaves drag her away. Talthybius gently takes the child, but, overcome by sympathy, he hands the child to his men. He will execute the orders of his superiors but he cannot look on while the innocent child is killed.

Again we believe that nothing more terrible can possibly happen. What is there that's still worse that could happen? A strange lament by the chorus sounds out now over Hecuba, who has collapsed anew. They sing of the radiance of Athens. This is part of Euripides's intent. His audience must see, behind the laments of the stricken, the glorious polis that organized the kind of campaign of conquest that the Hellenes carried on against Troy. The play was performed in the spring of 415 B.C. A few months later, Athenian forces set sail on the ill-fated expedition to conquer Sicily.

The scenes showing the events up to this point have gradually been raising in intensity. Now it is evident they were only intended to set the stage for what is to follow.

Helen, the guilty, the source of all the woes pictured, must finally come out of her tent onto the stage. We might expect that she is to be dragged out, like all the others.

Instead of the sergeant herald, we now get the general himself, Menelaus, the joint author of the whole campaign, the husband Helen deserted to run away with Paris. He has Helen's death decree in his pocket. The purpose of the war has been accomplished. Thousands have had to die to achieve it. What glorious words have been presented to the world to justify this war.

But now the real motive for the war is disclosed. It was waged so that the injured husband could get his erring spouse back into his bed. He cannot live without her. Naturally, he will not admit that publicly. He is enough of a politician to use smooth phrases to conceal his secret wish.

Menelaus announces that the death sentence must be carried out at home in Sparta, not here in Troy. He pretends she must be put to death by the dependents of those who have fallen in the war. But we all know he will never have her killed.

Menelaus gives his troops an order to drag Helen out of her tent by her hair. Instead, she steps onto the stage unruffled, dressed elaborately, royally ornamented, more beautiful than ever before.

Now comes one of the trial scenes so beloved by the Athenian public. Helen is conceded the right of the accused to defend herself. Far from stupid, she uses arguments that Menelaus lacks the acumen to cope with. But Hecuba's indignation grows in intensity as she demolishes Helen's arguments, one after the other. She seethes with contempt as she confronts Helen. Helen tried secretly to steal over the walls into the Hellenic camp! The idea would make Hecuba laugh if she were not beyond laughter. When Hellas was ahead, Helen praised Menelaus. When Troy was ahead, Menelaus was nothing to her. Helen, indifferent to virtue, cares only that she be in favor with the winning side.

Hecuba recalls with bitterness how often she pleaded with Helen to ship out to the Hellenes and get the war ended. But the vain and frivolous Helen liked the adulation of the Trojans. Now Troy is destroyed, brave warriors have died futilely, and Helen, who should be in sackcloth and ashes, is preening in her finery. To Menelaus, she adds: "For Hellas, for your own sake, in the name of all women, kill her, obey the law!"

The chorus of Trojan women is quivering with agitation: All of Hellas is accusing Menelaus of cowardice for displaying such leniency to Helen. He must show his mettle by putting her to death for adultery.

Menelaus replies that of course she is to be stoned to death for violating her marriage vows. This is his big moment. He relishes it. He has waited ten long years for this. Helen throws herself at his feet. Now she is really afraid. Hecuba demands Helen's death. Menelaus laughingly says that enough has been said. Helen is to be taken to his ship. But Hecuba understands all too well: "Let her not travel in your ship."

The soldiers lead Helen away. Now that she is out of sight, it is easy for Menelaus to play up to his part. Helen will get her just deserts. And so, with this lie he stalks royally off, a weakling who has got what he wanted.

The women gather around Hecuba and sing. Zeus has abandoned the Trojan women. Does it not grieve him—this they cannot understand—to see Troy in flames?

The finale is pure theater. Talthybius appears with the dead child in his arms. The tempo is heightened.

OPPOSITE:

No American production of Euripides has met with the popular and critical success earned by Judith Anderson's *Medea*. In an adaptation by Robinson Jeffers, it has made its place in theatrical history. In portraying a woman of rare depth driven mad by being thrust aside for another woman, Miss Anderson gave a performance that theater lovers are not likely to forget. Produced by Guthrie McClintic in New York City, 1947.

NEW YORK PUBLIC LIBRARY, LINCOLN CENTER

The Trojan Women is considered unplayable by some because Euripides, out of horror for war, relentlessly presented man's inhumanity to man in one episode after another. In this scene Andromache (as played by Edith Wynne Mathison), who has seen her beloved husband, Hector, killed in battle and her country laid in ruins, holds her son, not knowing that the most bitter blow of all lies in store for her. Produced at the New York Stadium, 1930.

THEATER COLLECTION, HARVARD COLLEGE LIBRARY

In this scene from the Michael Cacoyannis film of *The Trojan Women*, Andromache (as played by Vanessa Redgrave) tries futilely to flee from Talthybius (as played by Brian Blessed), the Greek soldier who has been ordered to kill her child. The Trojan women in the background (Katherine Hepburn can be seen directly behind Vanessa Redgrave), having lost their husbands and sons and fathers in the long war, are doomed to become the slaves of the conquering Greeks.

Hecuba (as played by Eva Le Gallienne) sorrowfully holds her daughter Cassandra (as played by Sloan Shelton) in a scene from the National Repertory Theatre production of *The Trojan Women*. Cassandra, the virgin priestess, has learned that she is to become the slave concubine of the victorious Agamemnon. Hecuba herself, the great Trojan queen, will become the slave of the hated Odysseus. Directed by Margaret Webster.

On a Greek vase (ca. 460 B.C.) the craftsman presented
Orestes, still holding the sword with which he killed his
mother Clytemnestra and her paramour Aegisthus, sur-
rendering to the avenging Eumenides.

JUTTA TIETZ-GLAGOW; DIE STAATLICHEN MUSEEN, ANTIKEN-
ABTEILUNG, BERLIN

OPPOSITE:

In *The Alcestiad*, Thornton Wilder used the Alcestis
theme as a vehicle for presenting a confrontation between Apollo and Death. Invisible to all the characters
except Death, Apollo (as played by Will Quadflieg) is
experienced only as a voice by the saintly Alcestis
(as played by Maria Becker) throughout the play. *The
Alcestiad* has never been produced in America. Produced
at Deutsches Schauspielhaus, Hamburg, in 1958. Directed
by Rudolf Sellner.

ROSEMARIE CLAUSEN, HAMBURG, GERMANY

His men will dig the grave while the women prepare his body for burial. Hecuba calls the child's death pure murder. The epitaph on his grave will be that a child was killed because the Hellenes feared him. It will be "an epitaph that spells the shame of Hellas!"

While trumpets blare the signals, the rising noises of embarkation fill the stage. Troy has been set afire. In the theater of Dionysus twenty-four hundred years ago, the light of flaming torches, clouds of smoke, the thunder and uproar of collapsing houses, were supplied from the Acropolis, lying immediately above the amphitheater. When Hecuba, according to the stage direction, tries to fling herself into the flames, she does so into the orchestra space, from which the soldiers drag her away. The slaves herd the women of the chorus into the ships. Hecuba must be carried off almost bodily. Into bondage to Odysseus she goes.

In the past this play was not highly considered. It used to be said that it was "A series of stage pictures, tiresome piling-up of outrages." Opinions have changed since the two world wars.

After World War I, Franz Werfel's adaptation of *The Trojan Women* was often played. The most recent version is Sartre's adaptation, *Les Troyennes*, produced in 1965.

Hecuba

Ten years earlier, in 425 B.C., Euripides had written a play about Hecuba. It has been preserved, but it is not one of his great works. The disproportion between the two halves of the play is too obvious.

The theme of the first half is the same as that of *The Trojan Women*. Of timeless relevance, it centers on the senseless sacrifice of the maiden Polyxena, another Iphigenia. She confronts Odysseus and triumphs over the ice-cold arrogance of the practical politician. So she goes proudly to be killed on Achilles's grave, another sacrifice for a favorable wind.

The women whom Hecuba has sent to the shore to fetch water for washing the dead girl's body for burial find a body washed up by the sea. It is Hecuba's youngest son, Polydorus, whose ghost in Hades had spoken the prologue to the drama. After the fall of Troy Polydorus had been coolly murdered by Polymestor, the friend whom King Priam had sent him to for safekeeping during the Trojan War. Polymestor killed the boy to get the gold Priam had sent with him.

The punishment of Polymestor is the subject of the second half of the play. Hecuba exacts from Agamemnon his acquiescence to her plan to avenge the murder of her son, though he is overcome with horror when he realizes what the old woman is capable of.

Under a pretext Polymestor is lured to Troy with his children. He does not know that the body of his murdered ward, which he thought was well hidden, has been found. He greets Hecuba with false cordiality, but he has hardly entered her tent before he is set upon by the women, who kill his children and blind him. He crawls out of the tent on all fours, roaring like a wounded beast. It is a scene of horror. Though Agamemnon is appalled, he must agree that the terrible old woman has right on her side. Polymestor is to be isolated on a desert island. Paralyzing horror.

Suddenly Agamemnon lifts his head. The wind is blowing. As in *The Trojan Women*, the women go off—into slavery.

Andromache

The play about Andromache was written earlier than *Hecuba* was. It is a magnificent sketch. Drawing its themes from a variety of mythological sources, it defies our comprehension just as it must have impressed the Hellenes of its own time.

Once again, years after the fall of Troy, the struggle between the house of Atreus, the Atrides, and the house of Peleus, the Pelides, is renewed. Andromache has been brought to Phthia, the land of Peleus, as a concubine for Neoptolemus, the son of Achilles. She has borne him a son. But reasons of state compelled Neoptolemus to marry Hermione, daughter of Helen and Menelaus, king of Sparta and son of Atreus. Both Neoptolemus and Hermione are only children. An alliance between Sparta and Phthia could make for a great power factor in Hellas. The will of the gods, however, is that Hermione be barren.

When Neoptolemus undertakes a pilgrimage to Delphi to placate the obviously angered Apollo, the domestic strife between the childless queen and the unwed mother rises in intensity. Hermione has sent for her father, Menelaus, to come from Sparta to Phthia.

When the play opens we see Andromache clinging as a suppliant to the consecrated statue of Thetis, mother of Achilles, in front of the palace. She is in the deepest distress. Hermione, appearing in majestic magnificence, threatens her in vain. Andromache has sent for the aged Peleus, who, as she knows, was opposed to his grandson's marriage to Hermione.

Menelaus has come and has proposed a plan. He gets possession of Andromache's child, who had been hidden away. Now he comes on with the little boy. He threatens Andromache: either she leaves the sanctuary and allows herself to be killed, or the child will be killed before her eyes. The mother leaves her place of sanctuary. Both she and the child are taken into the palace to be prepared for the execution of one of them.

Menelaus and Hermione are cynical enough to be indifferent to their promise. The death of the boy, who is a possible heir to the throne of Phthia, was their objective all along. The execution detail is actually under way when Peleus appears at last.

In a sweeping argument Peleus characterizes the old hatred between the house of Atreus and the house of Peleus as madness. His reasoning averts the execution. Menelaus now realizes that his will cannot prevail in a land where he is a stranger without troops, in the face of a hostile population. He decides to bow out and gloomily departs from the scene. He leaves his daughter Hermione behind in despair.

The second half of the play begins as we see

Hermione, now dressed in tatters, frantic with fear of what Neoptolemus may do to her when he returns and finds out that she had tried to kill his son. She is about ready to kill herself, when unexpected help arrives. It is none other than Orestes, to whom she was promised in marriage before Menelaus forced her to marry Neoptolemus. Neoptolemus is dead, and Orestes has come to claim her. They immediately leave together. The cortege carrying the corpse of Neoptolemus arrives. It is followed by a messenger who reports on what has happened. Neoptolemus was brutally assassinated in Delphi by hired thugs.

The Atrides have extinguished the line of the Pelides. Only Peleus is left. He grieves that "his lineage, his polis, all" has come to an end.

Thetis appears ex machina to forecast what is to happen. Peleus will enter into eternal bliss. Andromache and her child will be happy again in another land.

The tragedy exposes the sins of the mighty, the hatred of families for each other, the roots of evil. How trifling the grounds for all this seem, when measured by their consequences! It will probably always be so, as it was in Troy, in Phthia, in Delphi.

Heracles

Heracles, the son of Alcmene, was begotten by Zeus when he entered Alcmene's bed in the guise of her husband, Amphitryon. For that reason Heracles was persecuted by Zeus's jealous wife, Hera. She condemned him to serve King Eurystheus, king of Mycenae and Tiryns, and he performs a series of difficult labors in that service, the last of which has been completed. He descended into Hades and brought Cerberus, the hound of hell, up from below because his taskmaster wished to see him. Since then Heracles has not been heard of. Many believe he must be dead. Among these are the people of Thebes, the kingdom ruled by Creon, whose daughter, Megara, Heracles had married. Megara and her children live in the royal palace in Thebes with Creon and Heracles's parents, Amphitryon and Alcmene.

Lycus, a pretender to the throne of Thebes, has been summoned by his supporters to return from exile. In the bloody revolution that follows Creon is

killed. The new faction in power drives the family of
Heracles out of the palace. Not content with that,
the usurpers have decided they must liquidate these
silent reminders of the legitimate ruler.

The frightened, endangered family is clinging to
the altar of Zeus outside the palace for sanctuary.
There they are found by the chorus of feeble old men
of Thebes. Leaning on their sticks bravely, they have
come to show their loyalty to the old regime, but
they are powerless to help.

Lycus follows them closely at the head of his
forces. He does not dare to violate their privilege of
sanctuary, but he knows how to get rid of the sup-
pliants at the altar. Smoke them out! Already soldiers
are rushing to gather logs to build a fire for this purpose. At this, Megara, old Amphitryon, and the children decide to abandon the altar. They are granted
one last request; they can say farewell to the palace,
and the children are to be adorned ritually for their
march to death.

Amphitryon, in impotent fury, flings blasphemies
at Zeus: he is unjust; he does not watch over those
who need his protection. The chorus wails a lament
for Heracles, as for one dead. The procession of
those doomed to die appears from the palace. Weeping, Megara says good-bye to her garlanded children
and calls for Heracles to save them. Old Amphitryon
lifts his arms to heaven but lets them fall again. He
has prayed for aid too often in vain. One's life is a
feather tossed indifferently by the wind.

Then an uncanny event occurs. Megara sees him
first. Is it a ghost? Heracles! Warned by evil omens,

he has sneaked back into Thebes. He is silently approaching now, like a specter.

The armed soldiers scatter when they catch sight of the fabled hero. Who would dare to offer resistance to Heracles? He tears the funereal garlands from the heads of his and Megara's children. His rage at the threat to their lives is immense. The frightened children cling to his cloak. He roars in fury when he sees how deeply the fear of death still terrifies them. Prizing their love above everything, he comforts them even before he leads his family into the palace to await the coming of the usurper.

Lycus appears and is craftily lured into the palace. In a moment his death cries cut across the singing of those waiting impatiently for release. Then their ecstatic shouts of joy overflow the stage.

The music ceases suddenly. The chorus of old men scatters in apprehension. Ghostlike specters emerge from the darkness to give warning that, according to Hera's design, something terrifying will soon take place. The witch of hell enters the house to carry out her orders. Presently a messenger dashes out to announce terrible calamity. Heracles has murdered his wife and her children in the palace. (There could be a natural explanation for this: the intoxication and blood lust into which the assassination of Lycus plunged Heracles have robbed him of his reason and driven him insane.) Finally a crash in the palace wall brings stones tumbling down. One of them crushes Heracles, rendering him unconscious just as he was aiming an arrow at old Amphitryon. His limp body is bound up to one of the columns. The principal door opens.

The platform (eccyclema) described in my chapter on the theater of Athens is rolled out. It presents a frightful picture. The blood-spattered hero is roped to the broken stump of a palace column, asleep, with the corpses of his children leaning on him and his dead wife at his feet. Beside them old Amphitryon has his head hidden in his cloak. There is a song of lamentation, with a measured, mournful dance. It is a melodrama of despair.

Heracles wakes. Slowly he takes it all in. Amphitryon releases the bonds that confine him. There is an interval of silence. Then Heracles speaks a few verses in which he announces his intention to kill himself.

At this point Theseus arrives with armed men. His coming is not unexpected. Heracles has told us he has saved Theseus's life. When rumors of the coup d'état in Thebes reached Athens, Theseus decided that he must hurry with an army to offer aid to Heracles.

Heracles hides his head in his robes and waves Theseus aside. This is the turning-point of the plot. Solemnly uncovering the blood-stained head of Heracles, Theseus tells him that suicide is no solution for a Heracles. Hellas could never reconcile itself to such a death of one who was its benefactor and had done good for all mankind.

Heracles cries out that Hera has worked her will. Who, he asks bitterly, can be expected to play to gods who behave as she has done? Theseus's answer is that even the gods are governed by fate and must obey its law.

But Heracles is not persuaded by Theseus's reasoning. Another thought takes possession of him: one who has suffered such hardship as he has must undergo this additional adversity. Hera must not be allowed to laugh at him. Without guilt himself, he will live with the knowledge of the horror he has been through. He says good-bye to his father and his dead children. He puts his hand on Theseus's shoulder, and the two friends leave the stage.

The play is an uninterrupted sequence of horrors. No other play of Euripides, except *The Bacchae*, presents so relentlessly such a chain of dire events. Today we cannot imagine the shock it must have aroused in contemporary audiences. The murder of the children existed in the myth. Euripides was the first to set it at the ending of the tragedy, possibly presenting it as the last of the labors of Heracles; he was the first to present these events as following immediately Heracles's trip to the underworld. In many versions of the myth, Heracles is condemned to perform the labors as punishment for having murdered his children.

To the audience Euripides's message was: You who believe the labors of your beloved hero were a punishment ordained by a goddess on one innocent because of the guilt of a god must also believe that this goddess would punish that innocent one again and forever.

For this is the way of human existence. It has no meaning if it is intertwined with the will of the gods. It becomes all the more absurd to the extent that it is ruled by the will of the gods.

The Children of Heracles

This tragedy was produced a number of years before *Heracles*, possibly during the life of Pericles (who died in 429 B.C.). This story is a page in a patriotic textbook. It is reset in perspectives in which myth, miracle, history, and the present are curiously intertwined.

Eurystheus, the bad man of the Heracles legend, has prolonged his malicious pursuit of Heracles after Heracles's death, by continuing to persecute Heracles's young children. He has ample reason to fear them, for he knows they have designs on his throne. To escape him, the children are continuously in flight, accompanied by their grandmother Alcmene and by old Iolaus, a former companion-in-arms of their father.

No country is willing to offer them asylum. All fear the power of their pursuer. Even now, he stands on the border of Athens with his army, demanding

that Athens surrender the refugees to him. For their
part, they are hoping to win sanctuary at a temple of
Zeus outside the city of Athens. Without respecting
the sovereignty of the kingdom, a herald sent by
Eurystheus is endeavoring to get hold of the refugees
and take them into his custody.

Athenian citizens, attracted by the refugees' cries
for help, intervene. Then the sons of Theseus, who
rule Athens jointly, appear on the scene. When the
herald is ordered to give way, he threatens war. This
is a matter that must be decided by an assembly of
the people. There the kings prevail only partially.
Obeying the mandate of that body to resist Eurystheus, the kings must comply with a proviso demanded by the seers who were consulted. Possibly
manipulated, the seers prescribe that an Athenian
maiden be sacrificed to assure victory.

The Athenians can hardly be blamed for being unwilling to offer one of their maidens to be killed. At
this point, a daughter of Heracles comes to the fore.
She is Macaria, one of the Iphigenia-like heroines so
dear to Euripides. She goes willingly and proudly to
her death.

Thus there is war. An older son of Heracles comes,
with his army, to aid the Athenians. When the trumpets blow the call to battle, old Iolaus cannot bear to
be left behind. In a ludicrous scene he has himself
fitted with armor and weapons. He totters valiantly
into the fray as of old, supported on the arm of a
soldier. Then a miracle occurs. Mysterious powers
come to his aid. It is he who personally subdues
Eurystheus and takes him captive.

The closing scene belongs to Alcmene, the aged
grandmother. Herself at the brink of death, she con-

fronts her family's enemy. Eurystheus is entirely divested by Euripides of his traditional character in the myths. Regally he stands in his fetters, speaking like a thinker, one who has suffered. He says that he has acted out of fear, that his crown would sit uneasily on his head so long as the children lived out of his reach. Would Heracles himself, he asks, if Heracles stood in Eurystheus's place, not have pursued the children similarly?

But Alcmene is merciless. Though she is violating the very humanity that has saved her, by means of the aid of Athens, she gives the order for Eurystheus to be executed. The right of a prisoner to his life is just as sacred as the right of a suppliant to sanctuary. But the myths have to be adhered to in drama, so his death was demanded.

The Phoenician Maidens
and
The Suppliant Women

We come now to two plays that can be considered together. *The Phoenician Maidens* presents the events that precede *The Suppliant Women*. The basic motif of *The Phoenician Maidens* is the protecting power of the Athenian polis to shield the women in *The Suppliant Women*.

The Phoenician Maidens, produced about 410 B.C., toward the end of Euripides's life, embraces the entire Oedipus legend, from the time of the Sphinx and the murder of Oedipus's father, through Antigone's act of protest, to the last pilgrimage of Oedipus, the blind beggar. Knitting the whole story together, it compresses all the events into a span of a few hours.

The feud between the sons of Oedipus—Eteocles and Polyneices—in which they both die—is placed by Euripides in the center of the action of *The Phoenician Maidens*. In the background is the campaign of the Seven against Thebes, which Aeschylus previously portrayed in an extant tragedy. His play recounts the invasion of an enemy army into a peaceful country, which succeeds in repulsing the aggressors.

The theme of *The Suppliant Women*, produced probably about 421 B.C., is the refusal of the Thebans to permit ritual funeral rites for the bodies of the losers, which have been left unburied on the field of battle, to be devoured by scavenger birds. In this play, the mothers of the dishonored dead appear in front of the temple in Eleusis, appealing to a god for sanctuary. They invoke the help of Athens in pressuring Thebes to permit them to exercise the privilege of burying their dead, which was respected by all Hellas. Theseus himself acts as spokesman for his polis.

Both are great plays, each in its own way constructed with the highest skill. It is no longer practicable to produce them on our modern stages, for the same reason that *Heracles* cannot be produced. They depend for acceptance on concepts that prevailed in their audiences but can no longer be assumed as accepted by contemporary audiences.

In my chapter on Euripides's life and times, I reviewed the contemporary outlook affecting the reception of the plays. For appreciation of these plays, an understanding of their background and of their mythological sources is indispensable. This is especially true of *The Phoenician Maidens*, in which these basic elements are treated in a manner at variance with the ideas current at that time.

The Phoenician Maidens belongs to that later period of Euripides's work, when he showed a partiality for a chorus that usually remained neutral in the action. The chorus in *The Bacchae*, as we shall see, is only superficially an exception to this development. Euripides liked to interpose between the events on the stage and the audience the voices of essentially impartial observers, who, free from personal interest in the outcome, nevertheless take an interest in what is happening, voice opinions, and express sympathy.

It is such a chorus that gives *The Phoenician Maidens* its name. They are maidens from a Phoenician city on a journey toward Delphi. The prettiest girls in their community, they have been sent to perform services in the temple of Apollo. They have been delayed temporarily in Thebes because of the war. Housed opposite the royal palace, they accompany the changing events as they occur by dancing and singing in barbarian, oriental style. This kind of choral action is further evidence that this play belongs to a later period.

Two separate prologues have already offered surprising speeches before the chorus makes its entrance. Old Jocasta, a queenly matron, opens the play. (In this play, Euripides presents Jocasta as having survived the tragic discovery that her husband, Oedipus, is also her son. The blind old Oedipus is also still living.) She is the central figure in the plot. She wears the black garments of mourning, with her silver locks shorn short. She has lived through much sorrow. She towers above the quarrels and the hatreds of men.

Euripides gives the audience a shock by transforming the traditional character of three of the principals. Eteocles, the defender of his country, one of the tragic heroes in Aeschylus's dramas, is unmasked here as a cynical power-hungry politician. Polyneices, on the other hand, appears in a more conciliatory light, though it soon becomes evident that this is only a thin veneer concealing an equally egotistical determination to rule.

Jocasta speaks for the higher ideals of the polis as a whole. She reprimands both for their narrow viewpoint. She tries to analyze their motives. What is power? she asks. What is wealth? The gods gave it and the gods will take it away. She maintains that Polyneices, who has brought an invading army from Argos into Thebes to pillage it, is no more guilty than Eteocles, who has refused to honor the agreement that the throne will alternate annually between them. Fruitlessly, she warns that justice, morality, and reason cannot win out in this fraternal battle. Blindness to the other's point of view is the worst that can befall two in strife, she says. But the quarrel takes its preordained course. Eteocles proceeds to arm his men.

The audience is given another surprise at the entrance of the aged prophet Tiresias. He proclaims that the war should by no means be blamed on the sins of Oedipus, but on a sin committed against Ares, the god of war, by Cadmus, the founder of Thebes, who killed Ares's dragons.

Tiresias prophesies that if Thebes is to avoid destruction, a son of one of its noblest families must be offered as a sacrifice to Ares. He designates Menoeceus, the youngest son of Creon, Jocasta's brother, as the one to be slain. In this manner, Euripides turns the traditional myth upside down. The threat of misfortune is visited upon Thebes, not because of the guilt of Oedipus, the innocent victim whose sons are being visited by the curse pronounced against him, but because of an act connected with the very founding of Thebes.

Creon, crushed by the prophecy, tries his best to save his son from this fate. But the son, another Iphigenia-like character of idealistic youth, makes the supreme sacrifice for his country by throwing himself onto the pyre.

A messenger brings a bulletin of the progress of the war. He reports both a victory and an armistice. Arms have been laid down by both sides, and the suspension will be followed by a duel between the two brothers. Jocasta cannot permit such a catastrophe. With Antigone she storms out to throw herself between the two enraged combatants.

A second messenger brings a report that is a masterpiece of the art of tragedy. He describes the tragic end of the feud. The brothers have killed each other. Jocasta drew the sword of Eteocles out of the body of Polyneices and plunged it into her own throat.

Three biers are carried in. Beside them a fourth is set down. In it will lie the body of Creon's son. Over this Creon, in a state of collapse, bows down. Antigone now makes her great lament of mourning.

One of the principals is still alive. It is the blinded Oedipus, now free after having been shut up in the palace by his sons. Servants guide the living corpse, as Oedipus describes himself, onto the stage. He echoes Antigone's lament in his quavering voice.

Now Creon rises to take the crown of Thebes that has fallen to him. He forbids formal burial for Polyneices and orders banishment for Oedipus. Antigone, who is betrothed to Creon's oldest son, Haemon, disobeys this mandate. She will never marry Haemon. She will see that Polyneices is buried honorably, and then accompany her father into exile. Creon is unable to force her to obey him. Three biers are carried into the palace. The fourth, that of Polyneices, follows the aged Oedipus, who is led out of the city by Antigone.

The Phoenician maidens are now free to resume their journey to Delphi.

It is told in *The Suppliant Women* that each year the highest dignitaries of Athens and many of its distinguished citizens make a pilgrimage to the sanctuary in Eleusis to take part in the Eleusinian mysteries on the holy night of the goddess Demeter. This time, a procession of mothers from Argos has also arrived at the sanctuary to beg Athens to intervene on their behalf so that the bodies of their sons, left shamefully unburied outside Thebes, might be recovered and brought back for formal burial. Aethra, mother of Theseus, king of Athens, is there to pray to Demeter, the great mother, who is one of the Eleusinian divinities. Moved by the plea of the suppliant mothers, she makes herself their spokesman to appeal to her son and to the polis of Athens.

A herald arrives from Thebes to forbid Athens, in the name of Creon, to allow the presence of the delegation of mothers and to demand their immediate expulsion. Theseus, with the approval of his people, rejects this demand in the name of his polis. The legal situation is clarified: Thebes has no right to prohibit any actions of Athens. Athens had nothing to do with the recent war in which the Argive leaders were killed. In any case, Athens protests the violation of the funeral ritual in honor of the fallen dead, which is recognized throughout Hellas.

Theseus issues his judgment: Let the bodies lie in peace. Dead men offer no threat to the people of Thebes. The dead warriors are to be returned to the women of Argos, or Athenians will use force to compel the Thebans to treat the dead honorably.

The result is war. Hubris destroys Thebes, as

earlier it had destroyed the Seven from Argos. The Athenians bring back the bodies of their dead from Thebes, their only war booty. Five biers arrive at the sacred funeral sites. Lamentations and orations mingle with the weeping of the desolate mothers. The two dead warriors not there are Polyneices and Capaneus. Polyneices had been buried by Antigone, while Capaneus had been destroyed by a bolt of lightning hurled by Zeus. Theseus himself speaks the funeral orations for these two. In the closing scene, the remains of the fallen are burned on funeral pyres behind the temple.

Now there occurs a moving event. The figure of a young woman appears above the roof of the sanctuary, either from the hillside above or from the gondola device of the stage mechanism. She is Evadne, the young widow of Capaneus, who has put on her bridal gown. She sings her story of lost happiness, of her longing for her beloved, and of the miracle of a love that even death cannot end. Crying out that she is celebrating a victory, she leaps into the flaming pyre. Her sobbing father is left behind.

The sons of the fallen leaders bring the urns in which the ashes of their fathers will be buried in their home, Argos. Athena, the patron goddess of Athens, has the last word. She utters a bitter prophecy. These sons will return to Thebes, she says, and wage war there again. (Her words come true, according to mythological tradition, when the war of the Epigoni, the descendants of the Seven, is waged. Then Thebes will be destroyed for the last time.)

Even in antiquity *The Suppliant Women* was regarded as a eulogy of Athens. That implies idealization of the facts. Indeed, the polis shown in the tragedy as real is idealized. But never, Euripides seems to say, has the real come so close to the ideal as the ideas of Athens became in reality.

An aura of sadness qualifies this beauty. Euripides seems to be saying: This is how it was once, and is no longer. But the faith of the sixty-year-old playwright still glows. This is how it should be, he says, and could be again. Perhaps we may not attain it, but let us try.

The Athenian polis here assumes the protection of human rights. The one crime that must not be allowed to go unpunished is the violation of human dignity, a right that is beyond the laws of the state. The domain in which the plea of a suppliant for aid is respected and the suppliant is protected is that part of our existence where politics ends. It is the domain to which mothers, among others, are always loyal. This is one of the shining beacons of the Hellenic spirit over thousands of years that point a way to us with utter clarity. At other times and places religions have often dimmed this truth in wrappings of mystery.

The Suppliant Women was first produced probably at the time when peace had been concluded between Athens and Sparta (the Nicias peace, 421 B.C.). The thesis of Euripides was approved by his fellow-citizens: Even if this peace does not last, even if the good fortune of individuals is threatened, even if mothers never cease to weep for lost sons, still we should do all we can for our polis. Let us celebrate its fame while we defend its ideals.

Electra

Many years have passed since Agamemnon, king of Argos and of Mycenae, home from the Trojan War, was murdered in his bath by his wife Clytemnestra and her lover Aegisthus. The guilty couple are reigning in Argos, but are not free from fear. Agamemnon's son Orestes, who, a child at the time of the murder, had been sent away before Agamemnon returned home, has grown up and now lives in Phocis. There he and Pylades, King Strophius's son, have become inseparable friends.

Electra, the irreconcilable daughter, waits in Argos for the return of her brother, Orestes. She hopes he will save her and avenge the murder of their father. Apollo, whose temple at Delphi is in the land of Phocis, has uttered an oracle that has been interpreted to mean that the son of Agamemnon will return one day and avenge this murder by committing another.

No other work of Euripides was written so completely in antithesis to what his public expected to see. The plot hurries from one unexpected development to another, from one surprise scene to the next.

The scene opens at a peasant's hut. In the early dawn a laborer is leaving home to go out to work in the fields. We learn from him that Electra was forced to marry him, although Aegisthus had planned to kill her. Clytemnestra had persuaded him to agree to this solution instead of adding yet another murder to their guilt. Their purpose was to prevent her giving birth to a child of noble lineage who might make a claim to the throne. But this peasant is not typical. Born to a good but impoverished family, he possesses the spirit of fairness.

He says he has not touched Electra as a wife. How, if he did, could he face Orestes when Orestes returns home? So he has lived this way for years under the same roof with the princess. Clad in a filthy peasant dress, her hair tangled, a jar in her hand, Electra steps out of the hut. She means to go to the well for water. The peasant protests that it is not necessary for her to do menial tasks.

Euripides shows little sympathy for his heroine. He pictures her as any human being would act after years of such a life as hers. No one demands that she perform the chores that could be done by a servant, but she insists on doing them anyway. She has worn her hair cut short for years, far beyond the requirement of the rites for the dead. She garbs herself in the clothing of lamentation. Nothing prevents her from wearing her simple clothes decently, but she insists on being seen in rags. All these years she has cried her misery to heaven. She has to exaggerate her immersion in her grief in order to justify the meaning she has given her life: waiting for Orestes.

In fact, Orestes has just arrived, together with Pylades. He is not the hero, brave even unto death, whom she expects. He has slipped into Argos cautiously, in the clothes of a traveler. He has already prayed in secret at his father's tomb. He hears Electra's lament from a hiding place.

The maidens of the chorus, peasant women of the neighborhood who respect Electra, have noticed the two strangers. The two young men now come forward, saying they bring a message from Orestes. How can Electra recognize the brother she has not seen since he was a boy? Is he coming, she asks. She is told that Orestes wants first to know how she lives and whether she dares to risk the murder of their mother with him.

Electra's answer is full of reproach. Her mother lives in splendor on her father's wealth while she herself lives in poverty. Aegisthus swaggers proudly, claiming that Orestes will never come.

Orestes is not yet ready to disclose who he is. The peasant returns home. With a gesture of instinctive hospitality he invites the two strangers into his house. Electra bitterly asks him how he dares to invite gentlemen to so humble a place. He answers calmly that men of noble birth will value properly whatever they can offer.

It is Orestes who, in a great speech, the greatest in the play, sketches the nature of true nobility. Nobility exists in a man whatever his wealth or ancestry be, and Electra's husband is a noble man in the truest sense. He contrasts the person who constructs an image of himself, sees himself in terms of this image, and wants to be seen that way by others, with the person who has no such ambitions and is just simple and modest.

Then comes the recognition scene offered in a manner that borders on the grotesque. Electra sends her husband to fetch Agamemnon's ancient teacher. He lives nearby in comfortable circumstances, and he is asked to bring some food and drink for the guests. He arrives in a state of great excitement. Passing by Agamemnon's grave, and paying it his respects, he has noticed footprints and locks of hair on it. He thinks Orestes must have arrived!

Electra rejects this as laughable. Then the old man catches sight of a familiar scar on one of the strangers. Still Orestes does not acknowledge who he is. Electra pays no attention to the old man's dawning recognition. It is only when the old man asks emotionally why the two are not embracing that Electra approaches Orestes slowly. She asks if he is Orestes. Orestes answers gently that he is. There is no sentimentality, no prompting by "the voice of nature." At last music is heard, but it is from the chorus, not the flooding of sisterly feelings.

When, at last, brother and sister embrace, it is mechanical. Orestes abruptly ends the moment, saying that such things as embracing, however pleasant they be, should be postponed. Turning away from his sister, he starts to plot out with the old teacher a plan for a surprise attack on Aegisthus. As the audience knows, Aegisthus is on an estate nearby, where he is planning to organize a feast at which Clytemnestra is also expected. When the discussion turns to her mother, Electra interrupts. She knows how she can lure Clytemnestra to the hut; word can be sent to her that Electra has given birth here to a child.

When everything has been agreed on, Orestes utters a prayer, in which Electra joins him. They invoke the father's spirit. Orestes is hesitant, but Electra prods him on. Electra will keep watch at the hut with the sword with which she will take her own life if the plan miscarries. After an interval occupied by a chant from the chorus, we hear ominous sounds as of conflict coming up from the valley below. Electra's first reaction is that her young brother must have lost courage. The women have to stop her from falling on her own sword. Then a messenger arrives. He announces victory, but what a victory! It was sheer assassination. Aegisthus, unsuspecting, had invited the strangers to sit down to the meal. At the carving of the roast, Orestes plunged his sword into Aegisthus's neck from behind.

Exultingly, the triumphant Orestes makes his appearance with the corpse. He has wreathed himself with laurel. Electra puts on his head a diadem she has kept through the years. He is still aglow with the fury of his blood lust. He orders that the bier be set down in front of Electra. It is for her to throw it to the vultures if she so desires.

But when the cover is turned back and the face is disclosed, the women shriek and Electra jumps in horror. Shuddering, she stammers that the dead must not be dishonored, or the polis will condemn them. Then she pronounces a funeral oration over Aegisthus that is more like a lamentation. Adulterers and murderers, Aegisthus and Clytemnestra have brought great grief to each other.

The body is carried off, not for the beasts to feed on, but to be hidden in a corner of the house, so that it cannot be seen by Clytemnestra, who is now approaching.

Orestes is the first to espy the queen's chariot, which is now drawing close. The following scene is played at a frantic speed. He cannot bring himself to kill her. Not his mother! It cannot be possible that it was a god who ordered him to do this. It must have been some spirit of revenge who spoke in the god's name. The chariot is here.

Electra has no choice. She must spur him on with the taunt that he is not acting like a man. She pushes him into the hut. He shakes her off, saying that he will do it. But how bitter that he be so trapped, how harsh that the gods have decreed he do this awful deed. Electra shuts the door behind him.

Two horses draw the ornate chariot to the center of the stage. Clytemnestra is enthroned in it, in all the pomp of power and wealth, surrounded by her Trojan slave girls. But what kind of woman is it who now descends from her chariot, weary and bowed down? Her slaves help to hand her down. Her decline is barely hidden behind her heavily painted white mask. She is no longer the raging woman of the myth. She is one who has suffered much. She is stepping out of the solitude in which she has shut herself up. No longer does she dare to show herself in the city.

As she now, for the first time, witnesses the squalor in which her daughter lives, she is touched. Electra runs up to her as if to lend her a hand, but Clytemnestra waves her away. They look stonily at each other. Clytemnestra sees nothing but hate in Electra's eyes. Slowly Clytemnestra begins to speak. She repeats the old story. She killed Agamemnon because of Iphigenia, and then because of Cassandra. By what right did he bring this mad woman home from Troy to share their bed? There was nobody but Aegisthus to help her.

Electra has waited long for this opportunity. She seizes it to speak freely at last: Clytemnestra is no better than her sister Helen. She won her lover by means of her wealth and power. She rejoiced when she heard the war was going bad for the Hellenes. Even putting this aside, Electra asks bitterly, why were she and Orestes sent away. Clytemnestra does not try to refute the bitter words. She only says that Electra is one of those children who love their father best. Some children love their mother more.

But now she wants a reconciliation. She regrets her deed, she admits. She let her emotions get out of control. But Electra does not respond to her mother's overtures. Clytemnestra is ruthless, she says. Electra admits that she is frightened at Aegisthus's rage. If Clytemnestra was truly repentant she would bring Orestes home. They enter the hut. The moment has come for Orestes to murder his mother.

The cries of the victim from inside the hut have hardly died away when the doors are pushed open. Two biers are carried out. Two blood-spattered forms stagger out behind them. Now a burst of music relieves the unendurable tension that has been dammed up. Orestes reels around the stage.

Now he is a marked spirit, damned for what he has been incited to do. He blames Apollo, who urged him to do this awful deed. He visualizes the dire picture of his future life.

And—this is the last surprise—Electra agrees with him. She beats her breast and waves her arms. She blames herself for the greater fault. She urged her brother on and coerced him into carrying out her wish. The death shrieks of her mother have driven her almost insane. Her determination to get revenge against her mother has collapsed completely.

The voice of the oracle has become an idle fancy. The voice of nature in both of them has come to the surface as the genuine reality. Compulsively they conjure up again the horrible deed. Clytemnestra had torn her robe apart and exposed the breast that once had nourished Electra. She had raised her hand to Orestes's cheek. Then he had covered his face. Electra had seized his sword and pointed it to the body that had given her birth, urging him to use it.

Orestes and Electra cover the murdered bodies. Electra says that she covers the woman who had killed her love for her. The chorus murmurs, as if unattentive to what they are saying, that the great sorrow of the house of Atreus has come to an end.

The final scene is the epiphany in a gondola with the twin gods, the Dioscuri, brothers of Clytemnestra, the blessed spirits, the guardians of ships and sailors at sea. They announce the prophecy: In Athens Orestes will ultimately be forgiven his sins, and Pylades will marry Electra, for, basically, it is Apollo who must bear the burden of this guilt. But Orestes and Electra seem to hear only that they have to part. A song of farewell follows. Never again will they meet, never again see their native city. Orestes asks that they mourn for him as if he were dead.

A film that Michael Cacoyannis produced in 1960, with Irene Papas as Electra, was faithful to the Euripides original, proving that this tragedy still has the power to move.

Helen

The Dioscuri, Castor and Pollux, speaking from the gondola, tell us that Menelaus and Helen have just arrived in Nauplia, the harbor of Argos, from Egypt, to which the gods earlier had transported Helen. The Helen who went to Troy with Paris was only a phantom likeness to the real Helen.

Euripides's *Helen* is full of departures that contradict the traditional Trojan myth: the legendary area, Egypt; the palace of Theoclymenus before which the tomb of his father, Proteus, lies; the whole plot in which Helen is ensnared.

Here she is, Helen of all people, at the sacred tomb, a suppliant, desperately defending her virtue against the importunities of Theoclymenus, the young barbarian king. And the shipwrecked mariner who comes creeping in, in tattered clothing, is, of all people, Menelaus himself.

They have only just recognized each other when a messenger, one of the companions of Menelaus, dashes in to announce that Helen has been seen being transported through the air. Now he sees her here in the flesh. Is it possible that Helen can fly? This converts the interplay of being and seeming into a comedy, one that rapidly degenerates into a typical satyr play when Helen's vanishing is reproduced on the stage.

The clumsy deception could never have succeeded were it not that Theoclymenus is madly enamored of Helen. He is happy to learn the news she is supposed to have received, that Menelaus drowned at sea, and to see Helen in mourning garments. He hears this wonderful news from a messenger, who is really Menelaus.

Helen agrees to marry Theoclymenus that very day if he will grant her one wish: to permit her to bury her drowned husband out at sea symbolically, in the manner she claims is the custom of the Hellenes. He consents to everything she asks and cannot do enough for her. Placing his newest galley at her disposal, he puts the messenger in command of it. He hurries away to give these orders.

Soon after, a courier exposes this deception and reports the successful escape, bringing the plot to its close. Theoclymenus dashes into the palace with sword drawn to kill his sister, the priestess Theonoë, who had abetted the escape of Helen and Menelaus. The Dioscuri stop him.

Apart from the fact that the Trojan War was waged over a phantom, an irony that the play pushes far into the background, the character of Theonoë is what gives this myth so much depth and significance. The escape succeeds not only because of the Hellenic stratagem that was practiced, and not only because of Theoclymenus's mad infatuation with Helen, but because Theonoë exercised her freedom of choice. They must put their fate in the hands of Theonoë.

Her brother, Theonoë knows, will see her as a traitor if she withholds from him the information that the presumed bearer of tidings of Menelaus's death is in fact Menelaus himself. Helen and Menelaus throw themselves at her feet. They present their arguments to her as though they were arguing a case in court. It is a great moment, the turning point of the drama, when Theonoë announces her verdict. Hera would wish her to save Helen. But Aphrodite (who is supposed to have enabled Paris to win Helen as a reward for being given the golden apple) would never allow the truth about Helen's being transported to Egypt and the substitution of the phantom Helen to be revealed. Thus a human has the freedom of choice between the contending goddesses. May Aphrodite forgive her, but she cannot do otherwise than decide for what is right and just. It would be unjust for her to act so that her brother's lust could be gratified. She must act in the spirit of her father's wishes. It was to him that the gods entrusted Helen when they transported her to Egypt.

This is the moment Euripides chose to let the chorus sing their great song against all wars. Men wage wars over phantoms. They try to settle their controversies by force instead of by reason. But that is the way of this world: blood and tears, sorrows, nothing but sorrows.

Orestes

We discussed the most important scene in *Orestes* once before, in my chapter on the life and times of Euripides. Only seemingly does Euripides contradict in the beginning of this tragedy the prophecies of the Dioscuri, who appeared in *Electra*.

Here Euripides questions his audience: What would you as Athenians have done with a man who murdered his mother? He answers his own question: You would have subjected him to legal process. You would have taken the precaution of ostracizing him, forbidding anyone to house him, feed him, or to talk to him. Then you would have convened the people's court. By this formal procedure you would have pronounced the sentence of death over him, as happened in the case of the people of Argos against Orestes.

This is the juncture of events in which we see Orestes at the opening of this play. He has killed his mother, Clytemnestra, in retribution for her murder of his father, Agamemnon. Wasted away to a skele-

ton, lying on a cot in front of the palace, driven by
emotional stress to the brink of insanity, subject to
frequent paroxysms, he is attended faithfully by his
unhappy sister, Electra, who will not stir from his
side.

All possible escape routes from the city are guarded
by the military so that an attempt to escape would be
senseless. Menelaus is in Nauplia. He had sent Helen
ahead secretly to protect her, the root cause of the
Trojan War, against the people's rage. She is now in
the palace.

Orestes dozes off after one of his attacks. Helen
comes out to talk to Electra. This of course violates
one of the prohibitions in the mandate of excommuni-
cation, which obviously she cannot know about. She
volunteers her opinion, which is that Orestes and
Electra are not guilty of the crime as charged, that
the god Apollo alone should be held responsible for it.
She proposes that Electra, though charged with the
murder of her mother, carry her sisterly libations and
offerings to the grave of Clytemnestra for her, because she herself does not dare to show herself in
public in Argos. Nevertheless, she agrees when Electra suggests that Helen's young daughter, Hermione,
who is in the palace with her, be sent to the grave
instead. Helen agrees and the girl departs on this
errand.

Menelaus arrives with his bodyguard. When asked
to help Orestes to be freed of the charges, he displays the reaction to be expected of him. He is eva-
sive, but he will do his best to persuade the assembly
to be lenient in judging Orestes. Then Pylades
arrives. He was banished by his father, king of

Phocis, for his share in the murder of Clytemnestra and Aegisthus. A true friend, he has cut his way to Orestes with his sword. He accompanies Orestes to present his defense before the court. The sentence of death is pronounced, but then moderated to permit the two defendants, Orestes and his sister Electra, to kill themselves. The melodrama now really begins.

Reviewing their grievances, Pylades throws out a suggestion that is seized upon by his friends with wild enthusiasm. He proposes they should take revenge on Menelaus for his coldness to them by killing Helen. Helen must die! Orestes will become known to posterity not as the slayer of his mother but as the man who killed Helen! All Hellas will honor him! If they must die, let them die for a worthy deed. To this Electra asks: Why then must we die? She introduces a new stratagem. Let us seize little Hermione on her return from her errand to the grave and hold her as a hostage whom Menelaus can redeem only at the price of our liberation!

From this point on, the play is driven further and further into the realm of the theater of the absurd. The chorus, composed of the same women we saw in *Electra*, must first dance in tense silence, then perform the dance noisily in order to drown out the cries that are expected to come out of the house. In fact, for a time we hear Helen's outcries. Even louder is the moaning of her oriental slaves. One of these leaps down onto the stage from the roof of the house, bringing a message of an attack on Helen. He screams and dances the message in terror in a scene that is truly grotesque.

More and more it becomes evident that Helen

somehow has given them the slip, though she thought she was being murdered. Orestes and Pylades pursue her slaves to shut them up. Orestes appears with drawn sword, but it shows no blood.

Meanwhile Euripides inserts a deception scene. Little Hermione returns from her errand to the grave and promises Electra she will beg her mother to rescue Orestes. Menelaus now returns from the assembly. The three refugees are in the palace, but the great entrance door is bolted shut from inside. He orders that it be broken open. While his soldiers are hammering and ramming the door, the chorus starts to scream. All present point to the roof. The three he is pursuing are seen on the roof, Orestes holding the point of his sword against the throat of the kneeling Hermione. Menelaus demands the release of his wife and daughter.

Now it is revealed that Helen is no longer in the palace, but Menelaus can get his daughter only if he helps the accused to escape. The glow of burning torches flashes up out of the inside of the palace. Menelaus can only give vent helplessly to groans and moans. Orestes gives the order that the palace be set on fire.

The moment for the deus ex machina has obviously arrived. None other than Apollo himself appears in the gondola with Helen, transported there by the gods. Since her unexplained disappearance out of the house, all comprehensible meaning has disappeared from the plot. The prophecies announced by Apollo sound totally unrealistic: Orestes is even to rule in Argos as king, and Hermione, against whose throat he is brandishing a sword, is to become his bride. Apollo promises that he himself will persuade the citizens of Argos to reverse their verdict.

Why did Apollo not undertake to do this long before? That is as it may be. The game is up. It was just a play.

Iphigenia in Aulis

The sons of Atreus, Agamemnon, king of
Argos and Mycenae, and Menelaus, king of Sparta,
have assembled a mighty force to make war on the
kingdom of Troy, in Asia Minor. Other Hellenic
kings with their armies have joined them. They are
determined to avenge the honor of all Hellas, which
has been impugned by the flight of Helen, wife of
Menelaus, with her lover Paris, a Trojan prince. Punishment must be meted out not only to her seducer
but to his country as well.

A fleet has been gathered in the bay of Aulis, outside the city of Chalcis on the island of Euboea. The
army is bivouacked in tents on the shore. But the gods
are obviously angered, for there has been no wind
for weeks. Indolence is eroding the fighting spirit of
the troops. Subversive discontent is beginning to
spread in the ranks. The leaders have met in secret to
take counsel. They have asked the prophet Calchas
for advice. He pronounced the sentence of the gods:

Agamemnon, the commander-in-chief, must offer his daughter Iphigenia as a sacrifice to appease the wrath of the goddess Artemis, whose sanctuary is in Aulis.

Agamemnon has agreed. But he insists that the decision be kept secret until he succeeds in tricking his wife, Clytemnestra, into bringing Iphigenia to Aulis. To do this he sends Clytemnestra a letter ordering her to bring Iphigenia to Aulis, where she will be betrothed to prince Achilles.

The scene opens in the gray of early dawn. There is a light in the commander-in-chief's tent. Agamemnon steps out with a letter in his hand. He awakens his trusted servant and orders him to set out at once and deliver a second letter to his palace in Argos. In this new message he orders the women to stay home. Under no circumstances are they to come to the camp, as the betrothal must be deferred. In their conversation he tells the servant about Calchas's advice and his previous letter. The servant is horrified and frightened that Agamemnon had consented to sacrifice Iphigenia and used Achilles so deceitfully. As the music mounts in intensity, a feeling of tension arises. The servant hurries off and Agamemnon returns into his tent.

Now the chorus of young women enters. They have come from Chalcis, drawn irresistibly by the military show, the ships, the tents, all those glamorous heroes, who seem like demigods to them. Standing before the tent of the mightiest, the commander-in-chief of all Hellas's armies, they name the glorious warriors who are gathered at Aulis. Odysseus and Calchas, however, are left out purposely by Euripides.

Menelaus now pushes Agamemnon's servant, whom

he has waylaid, on to the stage before him. Menelaus has broken the seal on the letter and is enraged against the traitor Agamemnon. The noise brings Agamemnon out of his tent. A violent quarrel erupts between them. Menelaus hurls stinging accusations at Agamemnon: that he had used manipulating tactics to win the top command; that he had become aloof and inaccessible when he got the power; that he had bewailed bitterly the lack of wind because he would be deprived of fame and glory; that he had been at first all too willing to sacrifice his daughter when he was told what was required. And now, what Menelaus sees as Agamemnon's weakness, will bring shame to Hellas.

Agamemnon admits that he came to his senses only later, that only then did it become clear to him that if Hellas truly demanded that he kill his own child, then Hellas must be sick. Some god must have driven you and all the troops mad, he says. But his repentance has come too late. His anger is useless now.

The situation is out of Agamemnon's control. A messenger announces that the women are arriving. Half the troops are hurriedly gathering to see Iphigenia. Rumors are swirling about the camp, one of which is that Iphigenia is to be dedicated to the goddess Artemis. It becomes clear to the conflicted Agamemnon that he can no longer retreat from his commitment—he has fallen into the hands of fate. He is under pressure from the camp and from the politicians, who have the ear of the mob.

And now it is shortsighted Menelaus who suddenly sees the problem in a different light. Reckless and foolish as he is, he swings around completely when he realizes Agamemnon's despair. Now he is ready to renounce the sacrifice of Iphigenia and turn his back on the whole Trojan enterprise and the recovery of Helen. As though the choice still remained in the hands of the leaders! But Agamemnon sees that the followers have become the masters, that the leaders must become the multitude.

The following scenes are played in the shadow of Agamemnon's deception of his daughter. The women arrive, joyful and gay, and are welcomed by the chorus. Iphigenia flies into her father's arms. He cannot conceal the gloom that fills him. A sacrifice is mentioned, but Iphigenia does not interpret this correctly. Exultingly, she promises to dance around the altar. Agamemnon sends Iphigenia into his tent.

Agamemnon then tries to persuade Clytemnestra, in a labored dialogue, to return home. His pretext is that her younger daughters at home need her and that it is unsuitable for her to remain in an army camp. Naturally, Clytemnestra refuses to leave her daughter. Agamemnon commands her to go but Clytemnestra refuses and retreats into the tent. What is to be done? Perhaps Calchas can help.

Young Achilles, as yet uncrowned by the fame still to come, appears before Agamemnon's tent, in the costume and mask of a glorious hero. He wishes to explain the difficulties to the chief: the Myrmidons, his elite guard, are about to mutiny. Suddenly he espies a wondrously beautiful woman, Clytemnestra. She tries to embrace the youth she believes pledged to her daughter. She attributes his withdrawal only to youthful shyness and talks about the betrothal. But almost immediately she is overwhelmed with shame, for Achilles knows not a word about his supposed betrothal. He rages that they have both been deceived and feels that his name has been abused.

The old servant reveals the full extent of the deception that has been practiced: Iphigenia is to be offered up as a human sacrifice. Clytemnestra throws herself on her knees at Achilles's feet, and he agrees to help her. He will try to persuade Agamemnon to relent. If he does not succeed, they will meet again at the altar. He will be there with his guard to rescue the girl.

Now in a bitter argument, things come to a head. Here we have the accusing Clytemnestra, the innocent victim Iphigenia, and Agamemnon, who sees no way of evading his duty, of escaping his fate. Clytemnestra taunts him with caring nothing about his family and lusting only for power. Iphigenia, holding her little brother Orestes in her arms, clings to her father's knees and pleads with him to think of his children before Helen and Paris, who mean nothing to them.

Iphigenia says: So sweet it is to see the light of the sun. And alas to have to die. Agamemnon's reply is not without its tragic greatness. It demonstrates that he knows he is faced with a fate he cannot control: He knows what sympathy is. He loves his children. Frightful to think that he has to do what he must do. This sacrifice the Hellenes demand. They are as men possessed. Should he not comply, they will do them all to death. He acts not at the bidding of Menelaus. Hellas it is that forces him, whether he will or not. Powerless is their strength against the power of Hellas!

Will Achilles appear in time to save her? Yes, he

stands by his given word. He storms onto the stage to tell Clytemnestra that the mob is shouting that Iphigenia be offered in sacrifice. They are determined to drag Iphigenia to the altar by her golden hair. He is prepared to fight for her life, but even his own guard threatens him. It is clear that he will be killed and that Iphigenia will be sacrificed anyway.

Now Iphigenia's great scene comes on. This is the moment when she comes into her own. The sacrificial victim becomes the victor: "It is for Hellas they wish to slaughter me? But I am willing to die for Hellas. Everlasting fame will be my portion. Troy's downfall and Hellas's freedom are in my hands. Why should I love life and live on in fear? I was born not to you alone, but for all Hellas! Let me be sacrificed! Let Troy's fortress be destroyed! That will be my monument forever, my marriage, my child, my immortality!"

Iphigenia has left the world of reality. The mob that is determined to slay her is converted in her imagination into a nation animated only by motives of nobility. She is in a paroxysm of ecstasy that knows no men nor the world. She is willing to die to win the immortality of legendary heroes. A beautiful spectacle, transporting her into the realm of the mystical.

This play was produced in Athens in 405 B.C., a year after Euripides's death, in a version whose ending was changed. In that year, one year before the fall of Athens, it could not be given as Euripides wrote it.

Iphigenia in Tauris

Iphigenia in Tauris was written a full ten years before Euripides wrote his *Iphigenia in Aulis*. Goethe's great drama follows the plot of Euripides fairly closely.

Orestes and Pylades have come to the land of the Taurians on a mission for the goddess Artemis. He is to seize the statue of Artemis and carry it back to Hellas. By this act he can expiate the murder of his mother, Clytemnestra, for which he is still being hounded by the Eumenides. Their ship lies at anchor in the harbor concealed behind a headland.

They press on inland in disguise, though they know that the life of every stranger in this land is sacrificed to the goddess Artemis. When they are captured by shepherds and driven in fetters to the priestess who is to perform the ritual sacrifice, they find themselves facing a woman who is a Hellene. It is Iphigenia, who had been transported here by Artemis to save her from being slain at the altar of Artemis in Aulis.

Euripides was the first to rate the offering of human sacrifice, whether by Hellenes or non-Hellenes, on the same level with barbarity. Unlike Goethe, he does not conceive of Iphigenia as a "pure soul." She hates the Hellenes, who agreed to slay her so that the fleet might be able to set sail for Troy, but at the same time she longs for her distant native land. Euripides's ending, too, is different from that of Goethe.

After Iphigenia and her brother have recognized each other—one of the most famous recognition ("anagnorisis") scenes in literature—Iphigenia devises a deception to aid the prisoners in making their escape. She pretends they must first cleanse the statue by washing it in the sea.

Seemingly, Hellenic cunning will triumph over barbarian simplicity. But a storm comes up that throws the ship with its fugitives and the statue back on the shore. As prisoners they are brought before King Thoas. He decrees their death, but Athena, as dea ex machina (not as in Goethe's play), appears and resolves the dilemma. Goethe, while elevating the play to the highest level of humanity, also reduced its tragic impact.

The Bacchae

Dionysus, the god ever old and ever new—
that is, the one who disappeared and returned again—
had set out to conquer the world. Asia lies at his
feet. In the south and the north of Hellas, he has
established beachheads. Now he is at the point of sub-
jugating the Hellenes. Unlucky Thebes is to be the
city in which he will start. He chose it not because
he was born there but because it was the city in which
he was insulted. Mythical time is the present time of
the play. Cadmus, the mythical founder of Thebes,
is still living. He is the father of Semele, who was
selected by Zeus to be the mother of Dionysus. As
god and begetter, Zeus appeared to her in the guise of
a stroke of lightning. So close did he get to her that
she was consumed by its fire. Around the flame is
hallowed ground. A tomb and sanctuary, overgrown
with ivy, stand near the still flaming city.

Semele's sisters disparage their dead sister. It was
not Zeus, they suggest, but a mortal who fathered
Dionysus. To avenge this insult, Dionysus has chosen

them, as well as all the women of Thebes, as his first victims. This is the state of affairs in Thebes when the play opens.

Young Pentheus is the king. He is the grandson of Cadmus, the son of Cadmus's oldest daughter, Agave. At a time when Pentheus has been out of the country, dionysian madness has taken possession of the women of the city. Leaving hearth and home, they have rushed into the mountains as bacchantes, celebrants of Dionysus Bacchus. Moved by the powers of the god, the older men have also joined them, as has the patriarch Cadmus.

But the polis is showing resistance. The men, led by Pentheus, reject the god.

"First the drum of the great mother begins to resound. The drumsticks begin their rattle and the resin in the torches of the goddess begins to glow. Then the host of nymphs rages in. They whirl and throw themselves around and stamp in ecstatic dance." This is Pindar's description of the cavalcade of Dionysus and his throng of followers.

The maenads beat their tambourines. Castanets clatter. Their heads wreathed with ivy leaves, clothed in fawn skins, carrying a thyrsus in one hand, a torch in the other, the maenads dance wildly around Dionysus. Dionysus has put on human form. His mask framed by long locks is that of a girl, as are his clothes. He is not only god and man, but also both man and woman. At the end of the prologue he tells the maenads to beat the drum resoundingly so that Thebes will see what is happening. He himself is going to the mountain to dance with the bacchantes.

The maenads are half women, half creatures, who

accompany Dionysus in his triumphal march. They have something strange and wild in them, for, as in every human being, the strange and wild are always latent and will erupt when unleashed. It has manifested itself in the women of Thebes.

The music, the dance, the singing, are barbaric. The new god Dionysus takes no account of any difference between Europe and Asia, between Hellenic and barbarian. He recognizes no difference between Tmolus, near Sardis in Asia Minor, from which he and his throng have come, and Thebes, in which he was born and in which he has now decided to found his cult.

The scene that follows, grotesque and laughable, is meant to be absurd. In bacchante costume, with ivy leaves in his hair, using a thyrsus as a crutch, old blind gray-haired Tiresias the prophet patters in. He is led to the front of the stage and calls to Cadmus. Cadmus emerges in a short cloak, with a fawn skin covering his spindly legs. Tiresias asks where he may dance. The elders have already submitted to the new god, who recognizes no differences in age.

Pentheus, followed by his armed guard, enters the arena. He is angered when he sees these two oldsters leaping and shouting. He wears the mask and costume of a young hero. His manner of speech is lordly, sharp, and, as one of his people says, all too regal. His gestures are rapid and authoritative. His personal courage and intelligence are unquestionable. He is said to be without moderation, but in which respect? Can a king accustomed to ruling his city with common sense be blamed if he refuses to tolerate the lawlessness that has broken out in Thebes?

Perhaps Euripides deliberately offers the scenes in which the older people offend, so that the good sense of the audience will denounce the followers of Dionysus. Where will this lead to if these goings-on are not stopped? And even if a god is behind all this, no polis can survive if such madness prevails. Tiresias and Cadmus, who have accepted Dionysus, have nothing to propose to solve this dilemma. Established civic policies no longer have any relevancy once this divine madness has disrupted the ordinary life of the polis.

Tiresias expounds the credo of Dionysus. The earth was barren, then Dionysus gave it moisture. He gave us wine to have with our bread. He gave us the madness of prophetic vision to add to our understanding, for prophecy is also a form of madness. Tiresias says: Great power has he over Hellas; belief in the power of man does not make for humanity. We men of age join in the god's dances because we are not so insane as to fight against him as you are doing.

Then Cadmus adds another argument that would appeal to every Hellene, no matter how absurd it might seem to us: even if this god turns out not to be a god, it is to the interest of the house and the polis to honor him as if he were a god. He says that whether or not the god be fictional, the worship of him is noble and honorable. So he takes the wreath from his own head and tries to place it on that of Pentheus, inviting him to "Dance with us!"

But Pentheus hisses at his grandfather to keep that wreath away from him. Only respect for the aged and for piety stops him from treating old Cadmus roughly. But the other one, the seer, the seducer—he should be punished. Immediately he orders demolition of the temple of the seer and a police raid on the stranger who has driven the women mad. Death by stoning is the final penalty he commands.

A motive emerges in this scene that will be of decisive significance for the further development of the plot. Pentheus interprets an "orgy" as being what we associate with the word today, as sexual indulgence to excess. The foreigner is leading the women astray, into unchastity! He is desecrating marriage vows.

Pentheus has no other explanation for the events reported to him and that he himself has witnessed on his way into the city. Some hordes of women have already been arrested and thrown into prison. When women have lost all inhibitions, it is only libido that drives them. This attitude is in line with masculine assumptions by which a woman is nothing but an object for satisfying the male's sexual needs. The polis was essentially a male state. The thought that a craving to achieve freedom was expressed in the dionysian revolt of the women probably did not enter the minds of men of the theater of Dionysus. In this opinion there is also something of the bragging of the man for whom a woman is nothing else but a piece of property that exists to serve the satisfaction of his libido.

It would be foolish to maintain that *The Bacchae* represents a kind of early *Doll's House*, a play with a purpose aimed toward the emancipation of women—but one of its basic themes is the conflict between the sexes. It is highlighted by extreme contrasts. On one hand, we are shown the unleashing of the irrational that is believed by some to be more deeply imbedded in women than it is in men. On the other hand, we see the hubris of extreme rationality. Men base their right to power, claiming to be the sole possessors of rationality, and lay claim to the right to rule society on this assumption.

In answer to Pentheus, the chorus asserts the reality of the dionysian credo in the framework of a song of praise to true wisdom. It prefers peace, the company of the muses and the graces, to the boundless self-confidence of arrogant rationality. Dionysus is worshipped here as the god of the common man, the majority, and those who oppose him are not only presumptuous but also lacking in moderation.

The theme is repeated in the development of the plot. True inner peace can be achieved only after the excesses of the dionysian orgies. Once the dark hidden powers have been released and relieved, life under the customary laws of society can return to the golden mean, the balance, the equilibrium. This may well be so, but one must realize that this is not necessarily the point of view of Euripides. It is stated as the view of the dionysian chorus.

The armed guards bring Dionysus in, in fetters. But they do not feel safe with him. He did not offer the least resistance. Beyond that, the maenads they arrested have gone free. The chains that bound them have dropped off, the locks burst open. It is witchcraft.

Pentheus opens the hearing. The answers of the defendant Dionysus as to his person are full of irony. They alternate cheerfully, some coming from Dionysus in his apparently human form, others from him in his actually divine character. The questioning is concentrated on the principal charge of leading women into unchastity. Dionysus repeats the defense Tiresias has already put forward, that a woman's virtue depends on her own character. It does not take an orgy to make a woman immoral. The fact that these rites take place principally at night is quite irrelevant. Vice can prevail equally by day.

Pentheus debates this with Dionysus in a cold fury. He demands to see this god but is rebuked: he cannot see him because he is ungodly. This is too much for Pentheus. Despite Dionysus's warning, Pentheus orders him locked up in the stables. His women are to be sent to the slave market or to the factories. Dionysus, broaching the problem of personal identity, warns him again that he does not know what he is doing or even what he is. The armed guards approach Dionysus cautiously. Smiling indulgently, he goes with them.

The chorus of maenads, surrounded by armed soldiers, weeps loud laments for the disappearance of Dionysus. What follows is a mystery but this is not, as was often later claimed, the entire play.

The sacred section of the play begins now. Its opening measures are ritualistic. It is in keeping with the paradoxical nature of the god that he should die and live again, depart and return, be killed and then resurrected. The maenads raise their lamentation for his disappearance to a lament for the whole world. This weeping rises to a religious ecstasy. At its height they hear the voice of the god from inside his place of confinement calling to them.

The music of their antiphony swells in volume. The earth trembles. Houses are heard collapsing. The flames on Semele's tomb flare up. All are thrown to their knees, maenads and soldiers. Dionysus appears in thunder and lightning. The sacred section of the play has reached its culmination. It is his epiphany.

Great glory surrounds the god. Splendor radiates around him triumphantly. He announces in fiery verses what has happened, how Pentheus, first panting with rage, was made a fool of and finally sank in a swoon.

Never was a god's revenge more cruel, contemptuous, and insidious. And never did a man resist a god with greater hubris. Pentheus staggers out of the house with sword in hand. Catching sight of the "stranger," he hurls himself at him. He commands that all doors be locked. A shepherd comes running. He reports miracles on the mountain. He has seen an idyll, full of modesty and morality. Pentheus's unjust suspicions and untruths are given the lie.

It occurs to the shepherds to capture Agave, Pentheus's mother, and bring her into the city in the hope of winning the gratitude of their master. This causes a fight. Like wild animals stirred up by an attack, the rage of the bacchantes is unchained. They begin to tear the cattle apart. They storm down into the valley, pour into the villages like enemy invaders. And when the peasants seize weapons to defend themselves, blood flows not from swords but from blows of the thyrsus. The shepherds beseech their king to accept this god, whoever he may be.

The tearing apart of animals is a ritual of the cult. Like Zagreus in the Orphic myth, who, after being torn to pieces by the Titans, was reborn of Semele, in the person of Dionysus, Dionysus himself is torn apart by the women so he can be born again. The Orphic rites included the tearing apart and eating of animals representing Zagreus, to account for the presence of both divinity and evil in human beings. Thus was the power of the god demonstrated at the same time through an epiphany.

But Pentheus is not yet entirely subdued. He insists on continuing to run amok. He refuses the shepherds' advice. He blusters that this bacchic frenzy is disgracing Thebes in the eyes of all Hellas. He orders his men to mobilize, saying that Theban men will not crawl to the altar of this god in obedience to the terrorizing acts of the bacchantes.

Was he not right? Could he tolerate all this merely because it was instigated by a god? Once more, and for the last time, man's rationality rises up against the irrational terror of the god. Dionysus warns Pentheus in vain that he will die if he raises arms against him. But since warnings do not stop Pentheus, it will take other means to overthrow him. Here the mystery part of the play comes to its ending.

Dionysus displays his power over Pentheus, the mortal, without even needing a miracle. It is the dark side of Pentheus's own character that drives him to his fate. Dionysus awakens it by projecting before Pentheus's eyes a picture that arouses his sexual desires in a wave of perverted lasciviousness. Dionysus promises Pentheus to take him to watch how the bacchantes are carrying on up on the mountain. He will be able to observe everything as a voyeur from a hiding place. Pentheus still calls out for his weapons, but Dionysus, with a cutting exclamation, encourages the self-acting ferment working in Pentheus. Little by little, it destroys Pentheus's reason.

Now Dionysus has him firmly in his hands. His scorn abuses him and puts him to shame. Pentheus, the most masculine of men, must dress in women's clothing, as no man is permitted access to the orgies.

He must put on his head the same wig with flowing locks that he has just been ridiculing Dionysus for wearing. He must throw a fawn skin over his shoulders and carry a thyrsus as a symbol.

As Pentheus objects that all Thebes would laugh at his appearance, Dionysus promises to conduct him through deserted streets. Pentheus darts into the house at once, "into our net," as Dionysus says with mocking laughter before he follows him inside. Dionysus says of himself that though he is the most terrifying of the gods he is also the most merciful. The female clothing will serve Pentheus also as his shroud.

The maenads, now clearly seen as votaries of Dionysus, sing the refrain with real enthusiasm. Man's wisdom counts for little as the dionysian always triumphs. Submission to Dionysus is extolled again, for it brings the happiness of the quiet in the home, of those that live content with what each day brings without yearning for more.

Pentheus staggers to his shocking end. In his women's clothing he dances like a maenad. Dionysus escorts him from the stage in this absurd costume. His madness is clear to all to see, but also its cause: lasciviousness. At last he asks Dionysus to let him parade through the city in his female finery because, he says, he is the only man who would dare do such a thing. Dionysus assures him that he is great indeed, that his fame will rise to heaven after the suffering that he will endure on this expedition to the mountains.

The maenads transfer their mountain orgies to the stage and repeat them. Gruesome become their dancing and singing. They call down death on the godless, the immoral, and the unjust. They will laugh uproar-iously when Pentheus dies.

A messenger brings news. Euripides does not spare us any of the horror he reports. We see the voyeur avid with eagerness to witness the unchastity of the maenads, hiding in a grove of fir trees. Dionysus him-self had bent down a treetop to earth so Pentheus could bounce up on it, so as not to be seen from the ground. Pentheus disappeared out of sight, and a loud voice called out to the bacchantes that the man who mocked their orgies is at hand. And as he spoke, the messenger said, A holy flame leaped up into heaven from the earth. The heavens stood still and the valley was silent. No leaf stirred and no sound of animals could be heard.

Then we see how the maenads tore the tree out of the ground, and, as Pentheus plunges to earth, how they fell upon him, his own mother in the lead, and tore him limb from limb. Each tossed the pieces to the other with her bloody hands. And Pentheus's mother seized the head, torn from the body, to impale it on her thyrsus. She carried it through the forest as though it were that of a lion killed in the hunt.

She is coming to the city. The messenger rushes away, not to see the horrible sight. But the maenads dance and Agave steps into the dance with her son's head on her staff, dancing and exulting with the rest. She comes to invite her father, Cadmus, to the feast. She will nail this captured lion's head up on the wall, so all the world of the polis can see the prize she has taken in the hunt.

The last step is the worst. Agave awakes from her

madness. Cadmus comes with the bier on which the severed portions of Pentheus's body have been laid and covered with a black cloth. The raving mother, still radiant, approaches it with the head still on her staff. Now all the cast, even the chorus, falls back from her. She realizes what she has done. Agave is annihilated. So this is the reward for submission to the god, the gratitude of the god. Cadmus whispers that Dionysus has destroyed them.

A gap follows this passage in the surviving manuscripts of the play, but we do have some clues as to how the plot developed. Agave speaks a long lament. She counts over the limbs of the son she bore and murdered. How can she bear to live on after this? Then Dionysus appears ex machina. Some of the god's prophecy has been preserved. All of them—Cadmus, Agave, and her sisters—must leave Thebes and go abroad. In vain Cadmus prays to their ancestor for forgiveness, pleading that angry gods should not act as vindictively as mortals do. The victims, weeping, draw away, taking sad farewell of their country, their noble lineage.

The Bacchae is not like the medieval mystery plays because two mortals rise up against the sacred rituals. The first of them is Pentheus, with his claim for the self-created order of men. Then Agave accuses the gods for punishing minor sins—like the defaming remarks the sisters made about Dionysus's mother, Semele—beyond all measure and with cruel craftiness.

What, then, is *The Bacchae*? It is the tragedy of tragedies. It brings out into the open and examines the old myths that were the stuff of the theater in older times, using the archaic arena, the costumes and forms that were familiar. Gilbert Murray said that it is bound more tightly by form than any Hellenic play we know. It brings together everything the models of previous tragedy contributed and distills out of them what remained relevant to its own day. It is the essence of the human condition as Euripides saw it in 406 B.C., after looking back over a long lifetime.

Its myth is interpreted as a representation of the contradictions apparent in every era. Dionysus is not the anti-Apollo that Nietzsche considered him to be. He is in the center between the opposite poles, not the god of metamorphoses, but the god of dichotomy. He is in the middle between man and woman, between Asia and Europe, between Hellas and the barbarian world, between heaven and hell (according to Heraclitus, his other name is Hades), between death and life, between raving and peace (mania and hesychia).

Dionysus is the one who disappears and returns, hunter and hunted, murderer and victim, life and death. The tragedy consists in knowing that these two aspects are different sides of the same manifestation.

Goethe considered *The Bacchae* to be Euripides's most beautiful tragedy. In his last years he was preparing to translate it into "his own beloved German language." But death overtook him before he could do it.

Cyclops
(A Satyr Play)

The eighteenth play of Euripides to come down to us is an authentic satyr play. *Alcestis*, though given as the fourth play in a tetralogy, is not an example of the satyr play traditionally offered as the fourth play. *Cyclops* probably belongs to a relatively late date. It contains the usual satyrs, a "father" Silenus, and a chorus of shaggy-haired, pot-bellied companions, each of whom wears a huge phallus dangling from a belt. They are a typical dionysian throng. They spring out onto the stage as soon as the third tragedy of the trilogy (and we don't know which one) has ended.

The chorus of satyrs are slaves of the one-eyed Cyclops, the giant Polyphemus, whom we encounter first in the Odyssey. Old Silenus has cleared up the vestibule before the giant's cave. The chorus returns from the pasture, dancing and singing with a herd of lowing cattle. The homeric wanderer Odysseus comes in from his ship, accompanied by his warriors carrying baskets and jars. They have landed on the island at the foot of Etna to replenish their provisions.

Old Cyclops, Polyphemus, finds these new guests highly welcome. He is tired of dining on roast lamb and venison. He yearns for some roast man for a change. Odysseus warns him in vain to be moderate and honor the custom of hospitality, but Cyclops shows himself to be an enlightened superman who has no prejudices and is restrained by no law or custom.

Exercising the right of the stronger, he seizes two of Odysseus's crew to roast them for a meal. The high point of the scene comes when Odysseus and Silenus get Cyclops drunk after his repast. When that happens, he is moved by lust to drag Silenus into his bed with him in the cave. This presents the opportunity of revenge. A wooden pole is sharpened and made red-hot in the fire. With its pointed end, Odysseus gouges out the one eye that Cyclops has.

The stage is filled with Cyclops's yells of pain. From a safe distance Odysseus, who had previously told him his name was Nobody, tells him his real name. While the chorus follows Odysseus to his ship to make their escape, the blinded Cyclops gropes his way along the rocky boulders on the coast and tries to smash the ship in his helpless rage.

EURIPIDEAN DRAMA
ON THE EUROPEAN STAGE

Of all the plays by the three great Hellenic writers of tragedy, those by Euripides became, soon after his death in 406 B.C., the most frequently produced. They influenced markedly the popular theater of the new comedy. Very soon his plays began to be adapted and revised, a fate they have encountered almost always, even today.

Themes, motives, characters, many of which he invented, have attracted other writers and constantly inspired new versions of his plots. In the later centuries of antiquity, touring guest stars would cite soliloquies from his tragedies and accompany them with gestures suitable to the action until the last ounce of expression was wrung out of the passages they chose.

The changes in public taste that developed in succeeding eras can be studied best by reading the dramas of the Roman dramatist Seneca. But even before the time of Seneca, a *Medea* was written by the Roman

Ovid. And even before Ovid, the founders of the Hellenic theater in Rome, especially Ennius, could not have succeeded without Euripides, any more than Plautus and Terence could have done without Menander, the master of the new comedy in Hellas.

Five of Seneca's rhetorical tragedies draw their themes from Euripides: *Hercules Furens*, *Troades*, *Medea*, *Phoenissae*, and *Phaedra*. They departed far from Euripides's originals and they, in turn, have served as models for further adaptations by others. Euripides was the only one of the Hellenic tragic writers that Dante introduced into *The Divine Comedy*. He was of interest to the Christian Middle Ages, not as a so-called rationalist, but because he was a critic of the pantheon of Hellenic gods.

It was the humanists who began to translate Euripides's plays, at first into Latin, as did Erasmus and Melancthon. They also inspired the presentation of Euripides's dramas in academic institutions. We have evidence that such performances took place in Strasbourg in 1567. There were others in Italy, Spain, France, and England. Some were given in glamorous settings, such as Andrea Palladio's Teatro Olimpico in Vicenza, that charming house constructed during the Italian renaissance especially for the revival of Hellenic plays.

Calderón probably became acquainted with Euripides through scholars who had studied him. Possibly Shakespeare did, too, though the unfaithful queen in *Hamlet* is more like Seneca's *Hecuba* than a character from Euripides. Certainly, Corneille, who wrote a *Medea*, must have been acquainted with Euripides. Racine wrote a whole series of epochal dramas for his theater, including *Le Thebaide* (after *The Phoe-*

nician Maidens), *Alceste, Andromaque, Iphigénie en Aulide, Iphigénie en Tauride*, and *Phèdre*.

There have been plays in German on themes from Euripides since 1604. In Copenhagen, Johann Elias Schlegel followed in Racine's footsteps. But the really important center was Weimar. In 1789 Schiller translated *Iphigenia in Aulis* and passages from *The Phoenician Maidens*. Ten years before that, Goethe had prepared a prose version of *Iphigenia in Tauris* for an amateur production. In 1800 he brought the drama in more felicitous form to the Weimar stage in a performance directed by Schiller. A year later, August Wilhelm Schlegel followed with a production of *Ion*, which met with only limited success.

In the early 1770s, Goethe wrote a gay farce entitled *Götter, Helden und Wieland* to satirize Christoph Martin Wieland, who had written a sugary version of *Alcestis*. Later, however, Goethe decided that Wieland's effort was not so far astray. *Alcestis* had been made into an opera, and Goethe himself now considered writing librettos for short oratorios in order to revive a dramatic medium in which chorus figured prominently.

In 1800 Goethe had Christoph Willibald Gluck's *Iphigénie en Tauride* produced in Weimar. At the same time he was working on the act about Helen in his *Faust*, using the original poetic meters of Hellenic tragedy. In this he was strongly influenced by Euripides. He was also occupying himself with a reconstruction of some of Euripides's lost works, including the *Phaeton*. In the last year of his life, he started on a translation of *The Bacchae*.

Nevertheless, not a single translation of any of the tragedies of Euripides seems to have been produced on the Weimar stage. Franz Grillparzer's *Medea*, in his trilogy *Das goldene Vlieβ*, echoes the Weimar interest in Euripides. It was presented originally in the Burgtheater in Vienna in 1821. For a long time this version diverted attention from the original itself.

Beginning in the nineteenth century, it was a growing interest in ancient history that attracted contemporary German poets to trying to reconstruct the authentic theater of antiquity. This led to the performances of plays of Euripides in the splendid Roman theater in Orange, beginning in 1899. This interest was enhanced by the astonishing archaeological excavation of Mycenae. That discovery cast doubt on the validity of Johann Joachim Winckelmann's epigram on ancient Hellas—"noble simplicity and static greatness"—and exposed the fallacy of August Wilhelm Schlegel's prejudice against Euripides as "the destroyer of tragedy."

It was then that Hugo von Hofmannsthal had his first encounter with antiquity. As early as 1893 he wrote *Die ägyptische Helena*; it was not published until 1911, when it was performed in the Deutsches Theater in Berlin. Richard Strauss used this play as the basis for his opera in 1928. He was also busy in 1904 with a sketch for *Pentheus*, which reflected his absorption in *The Bacchae*. He wrote his *Alkestis* in 1923 as a text for an opera by Egon Wellesz. Alexander Lernet-Holenia wrote an *Alkestis* in beautiful verse in 1927.

In spite of these, there was no noteworthy production of a play by Euripides on any German stage before World War I. It was quite otherwise in England, thanks largely to the work of Gilbert Murray. This great scholar began to translate the texts into

English in 1904 with profoundly scientific thorough-
ness. His editions are still basic for the study of Euripides. His work combines deep insight into the spirit
of the tragedies with poetic imagery fortified by an
artistic command of the English language. Through
his work actresses such as Sybil Thorndike have been
enabled to act the roles of Medea and Hecuba. T. S.
Eliot was stimulated by the Murray translations to
write *The Cocktail Party* (1949). He said that he had
patterned the character of Sir Henry after Heracles
in Euripides's *Alcestis*. There is no doubt that Thornton Wilder studied them when he wrote *The
Alcestiad* (which has not, however, been published or
performed in the United States). It was World War I
that turned the attention of the theater in Germany
again to the dramas of Euripides.

Franz Werfel had a presentiment of the future
when he began to work on *Die Troerinnen*, his adaptation of *The Trojan Women*, the play that had always been deemed unplayable as a "heaping-up of
horrors." He wrote the preface to his adaptation in
March 1914, opening with the line: "The translation
of this tragedy was occasioned by my belief that the
history of mankind proceeds in a cycle, and has returned to the situation out of which this play arose."
When the play was produced on the Berlin stage in
1916, the drama critic Alfred Kerr wrote of it: "This
shattering play by our contemporary, Euripides, resounds like a frightful requiem for our convulsive
present."

The expressionists had also discovered Euripides. In
1917, Frank Wedekind wrote a *Herakles*, his last play.
The *Medea* by Hans Henny Jahnn, produced in 1923,
was a Berlin sensation. Siegfried Jacobsohn wrote of

it: "The poet has been inflamed by a frighteningly vivid representation of our own epoch, rather than by a blood-thirsty fable of antiquity."

The adaptation of *The Bacchae* by Berthold Viertel in 1925 has been presented in numerous theaters. In his *Atridentetralogie*, Gerhart Hauptmann, now lonely and isolated in the dark World War II world, utilized the episode presenting an outbreak of mass hysteria in Euripides's *Iphigenia in Aulis* to reveal the sad reality of the contemporary world.

In 1957 *The Trojan Women* was brought to the stage again. Mattias Braun's Brecht-like adaptation deeply impressed theatergoers of the time. Jean-Paul Sartre's version, *Les Troyennes*, premiered in 1965, has been seen on stages all over the world.

Adaptations, adaptations! There is also Anouilh's French version of Mattias Braun's German *Medea*. Jean Giraudoux has offered us the outstanding French *Electre* (1937), and Sartre has adapted the myths of Clytemnestra's murder of Agamemnon and the subsequent fate of Electra and Orestes in *Les Mouches* (1943) to analyze the values of resistance in German-occupied France.

But where is Euripides himself? He is still played in his own tongue in the ancient theaters in Athens, in Epidaurus, in Syracuse, and in the Provence. But the productions have been stylized and prettied up too much in order to smooth over the provocative sharp angles in the original texts. Innumerable opera librettos, from Monteverdi through Gluck to Hans Werner Henze, have been based on his texts.

Looking back through my memories, I can single out two evenings that brought me close to the spirit of Euripides, both of which, unfortunately, filtered through the screen of another artist's interpretations. The first was when I heard Maria Callas sing Cherubini's *Medea*, an outcry of wild fury and a lament for all mankind. The second was another *Medea*, in a translation by Johannes Stroux, in which Maria Wimmer portrayed a woman drowning in the despair. Both occasions ended by converting horror into beauty, a formula that it seems to me appropriate to apply to much of the work of Euripides.

EURIPIDEAN DRAMA
ON THE AMERICAN STAGE

The plots and the characters created or elaborated by Euripides have appeared in many translations and adaptations by poets and playwrights in Europe, but they have not provided inspiration or models for writers for the American theater until comparatively recently. His characters, however, are well-known to all drama lovers. His women, especially, are well-remembered. Antigone, Alcestis, Electra, Hecuba, Helen, Iphigenia, Medea, Phaedra, the Phoenician Maidens, the Suppliant Women, the Trojan Women—these are names that call up pictures and situations that exist in the mind of every student of the world stage and its literature.

The files of the theater collection in the New York Public Library contain dozens of references to productions of Euripides in this country during the pres-

This chapter was specially written by Samuel R. Rosenbaum for this American edition.

ent century, but, with few exceptions, they have been well-meaning, rather than professional, efforts by enthusiastic scholars to bring Hellenic plays to life for the benefit of earnest students.

There is, however, the outstanding contribution of Margaret Anglin, who, from 1911 to 1927, gathered around herself a well-trained company of college-bred young professionals. For a number of seasons this troupe offered very creditable productions of Shakespeare and of the Hellenic tragedies in the renowned Greek outdoor theater Miss Anglin founded at Berkeley, California. Canadian-born, she came from a family prominent in the public life of the Dominion. She possessed scholarship as well as a solid theater sense in the best traditions of the British and American theater. Her productions of *Medea*, *Electra*, *Hippolytus*, and *Iphigenia in Aulis*, were staged with real distinction and public acclaim.

It has not been in the tradition of producers or actors in this country to risk investment or reputation with plays that might appeal to only a very elite and limited audience. It is perhaps only where the theater is subsidized that it can afford to experiment and even fail.

Judith Anderson, the Australian-born actress, was the first to bring Euripides to the American stage on a grand scale. As Robinson Jeffers tells it, she asked him in the early 1940s to write an adaptation of *Medea* for her. Although he had never before written a poem to order, he worked on this assignment, aided by "some invaluable suggestions by Miss Anderson, visiting me here in Carmel."

The play was produced by Guthrie McClintic in New York City in 1947, with Miss Anderson in the title role and with a distinguished cast of seasoned actors. It was an immediate and spectacular success.

Brooks Atkinson wrote of it in the *New York Times*:

> Medea is mad with the fury of a woman of rare stature. It is a part incomparable for passion and scope. She is barbaric by inheritance, but she has heroic strength and vibrant perceptions. Animal-like in her physical reactions, she plots the doom of her enemies with the intelligence of a priestess of black magic, at once obscene and inspired. She fills the evening with fire, horror, rage and character.

For two seasons *Medea* played in most of the larger cities of America from coast to coast. Everywhere it won the plaudits of audiences overwhelmed by the power of the drama and its presentation.

This experience stimulated a reexamination of other plays by Euripides. In subsequent years a number of them were produced in either amateur or professional productions, winning a fair degree of acceptance.

Hippolytus, with its marvelous Phaedra, had appeared fleetingly in the Cleveland Playhouse late in 1927. It was again presented in the Lenox Hill Playhouse in 1948, this time with a musical accompaniment composed by the young American composer Ned Rorem. *Hippolytus* was also offered in modern Greek by a company from Greece, the Piraikon Theatron, in the Felt Forum in New York City and in Chicago in 1948, but it naturally was of interest to few theatergoers.

A short-lived, off-Broadway production of *Electra*

was offered in the 1957–1958 season at the little Jan Hus Theater in New York City.

In 1961 and 1962 the Mermaid Theater offered a somewhat abbreviated *Alcestis*, entitled *Alcestis Comes Back*. Again it had a very short life.

It was soon followed, in December 1963, by a truly historic theater event: *The Trojan Women*, at the off-Broadway Circle in the Square theater. It was directed by the well-known Michael Cacoyannis, who had previously directed this play in Europe with resounding success, and produced by Theodore Mann. The play was presented in a beautiful translation by Edith Hamilton. The part of Hecuba was created by Mildred Dunnock. Her audience-hypnotizing performance filled the little 299-seat theater for more than six months. This production was made into a successful motion picture in 1971, with Irene Papas, Vanessa Redgrave, and Katherine Hepburn. It was a success d'estime, but its merit was not reflected at the box office.

The artistic and popular success of this stage production of *The Trojan Women* stimulated the National Repertory Theater to put on its own production in 1966, with the great Eva Le Gallienne as Hecuba. Offering a translation by Gilbert Murray, the Repertory production was directed by Margaret Webster. Performed throughout the National Repertory itinerary, it made a profound impression on American theatergoers. The case against war has never been made more eloquently.

In Philadelphia, the reviewer H. T. Murdock wrote of it:

Such is the power of this speech, which takes

the place of action, that action is unnecessary. The story of the woe war causes could not have been better told by clashing armies and milling mobs. Even while man has never done much to abolish its terrors, its cruelties, and the waste and heartbreak of war, he has, through the centuries, uttered his protests. Of all such expressions, none is more eloquent than this text of Euripides, written in 415 B.C., not to celebrate another Athenian victory, but to chide his countrymen for a cruel war of aggression.

The National Repertory Theater was a hopeful venture supported by generous contributors who provided funds to cover its losses. It was not able to survive more than a couple of deficit-ridden seasons.

In 1967 and 1968 Theodore Mann produced *Iphigenia in Aulis* at the Circle in the Square. In 1970 he took it to the newly reopened Ford's Theater in Washington.

The Yale School of Drama, seedbed of so many brave experiments for the stage, performed *Medea* in 1969 and 1970. The boldly experimental La Mama played this in its cellar on New York's East Side in 1972. This version combined the text by Euripides with a later version of the play by the Roman Seneca.

Then, in 1969, came another history-making production, *The Bacchae*, by the Yale School of Drama in New Haven. Using a new translation from Euripides by Kenneth Cavander, this complex, baffling play was directed by the controversial but highly gifted André Gregory. Julius Novick wrote in the *New York Times*:

Until recently this late tragedy of Euripides had not been widely read, and it had almost never been produced. The play is complex and ambiguous, but its story is essentially simple. The god Dionysus is opposed by Pentheus, the young king of Thebes. In revenge, Dionysus causes Pentheus to be torn apart by a band of crazed women, led by Pentheus's own mother. As Euripides here depicts him, Dionysus is, for better or worse, the god of our own times, the god of intoxication, of frenzy, of release your inhibitions and blow your minds, the god of freak-out, the god who makes you dance until the mind splits open and the world falls in, and is glad. We had better learn as much about him as we can. Our survival may depend on it. *The Bacchae* is being talked about more and more, and written about and produced on the stage. It has seen student productions at Harvard and Yale. It was done professionally in Boston last fall. The dominant figure in this production is Alvin Epstein as Dionysus. He neglects the easy joyousness that is part of what Dionysus represents, but he gives us the sensuality, the strangeness, the mystery, the threat, and the overwhelming authority.

The Bacchae had earlier been staged, in 1963, in Pittsburgh at the College of Fine Arts in the Carnegie Institute of Technology. Its score was composed by Elizabeth Lutyens of London, daughter of the famous architect Sir Edward Lutyens.

In January 1973 Minos Volanakis's adaptation of *Medea* was staged at the new, uptown Circle in the Square in New York City for a limited engagement.

The production, directed by Volanakis, received enthusiastic reviews from many of the city's major theater critics, who described Irene Papas's performance in the title role as "brilliant," "towering," "searing," and "formidable." But while he acknowledged Miss Papas's own effective resources, Walter Kerr, writing for the Sunday edition of the *New York Times* (28 January 1973), accused Volanakis of making Medea "more victim than *daimon*, more nearly hausfrau than maddened magician," and took special exception to the language of the adaptation—to the "commonplaces" that cause "odd clashes between image and text, between expectation and event. . . ." Aiming particularly at the device that was used to represent Medea and her children being spirited away in a chariot—a glowing, illuminated disc against the back wall—and at the "ghostly amplifier" through which the audience hears Medea's last lines, Mr. Kerr continued in his review:

> . . . the production as a whole is strange in its apparent randomness, its willingness to use devices without much thought for what they will *say* in the scene. Everything that is seen on the stage takes on meaning for an audience, whether the meaning was intended or not—which means that it had better *be* intended if it is not to play hob with what is really going on.

Professional performances of Euripides are not apt to be frequent. To prepare and present such a production professionally requires an unusual combination of sound scholarship, brilliant showmanship, well-trained acting principals (at least one of whom must be a woman of magnificent stage presence), bold financial investment, and lucky timing. Only well-meaning or well-heeled amateurs are apt to embark on such a venture, and they are likely to lack one or another of the qualifications necessary for success.

BIBLIOGRAPHY

Arnott, Peter. *Greek Scenic Conventions*. Oxford, 1962.

Bates, William N. *Euripides, a Student of Human Nature*. New York, 1930. Reprint, 1969.

Bieber, Margaret. *The Greek and Roman Theatre*. Princeton, N. J., 1961.

Bowra, C. M. *Ancient Greek Literature*. Paper edition. New York, 1960.

Conacher, D. J. *Euripidean Drama: Myth, Theme and Structure*. Toronto, 1967.

De Charme, Paul. *Euripides and the Spirit of His Dramas*. Translated by James Loeb. Port Washington, N. Y., 1906.

Hadas, Moses. *History of Greek Literature*. New York, 1950.

Jackson, John. *Marginalia Scaenica*. New York, 1955.

Lattimore, Richmond. *The Poetry of Greek Tragedy*. Baltimore, Maryland, 1958. Paper, New York, 1966.

Murray, Gilbert. *Euripides and His Age.* Second edition. New York, 1965.

————. *A History of Ancient Greek Literature.* Reprint. New York, 1966.

Pickard-Cambridge, A. W. *The Theatre of Dionysus in Athens.* Oxford, 1946.

Ritchie, William. *Authenticity of the "Rhesus" of Euripides.* New York, 1964.

Solmsen, F. *"Electra" and "Orestes."* Amsterdam, 1967.

Verrall, A. W. *"Bacchantes" of Euripides.* New York, 1910.

————. *Euripides the Rationalist.* New York, 1895.

Webster, T. B. L. *Greek Theatre Production.* London, 1956.

————. *The Tragedies of Euripides.* New York, 1968.

Wilson, John T., ed. *Twentieth-Century Interpretations of Euripides' Alcestis.* Englewood Cliffs, N.J., 1968.

Winnington-Ingram, R. P. *Euripides and Dionysus.* 1948.

Zuntz, G. *Political Plays of Euripides.* New York, 1955.

INDEX